To Christos

a fellow T...... —

of time long, long   ago

Charles Farrell

October . 2005 .

REFLECTIONS 1939-1945

A SCOTS GUARDS OFFICER
IN TRAINING AND WAR

The Squadron Colour.

'S' Squadron Colour
3rd Tank Battalion Scots Guards
Normandy to the Baltic 1944-1945

Major W.S.I. Whitelaw MC   Major Charles Farrell MC

Captain N.W. Beeson   Captain W.P. Bull   Captain C.S.R. Graham
(killed in action)

Lt C.R.T. Cunningham   Lt Richard Humble   Lt A.R.G. Stevenson MC
(wounded)   (killed in action)

Lt E.P. Hickling MC   Lt P.M. Ward   Lt T.E.P. Gilpin   Lt Michael Law

The letter 'S' was the next available letter of the alphabet when the Battalion re-formed
in October 1940 – it does not denote 'support' as has sometimes been believed.

Reflections 1939-1945

A Scots Guards Officer
in Training and War

by

Charles Farrell

The Pentland Press Limited
Edinburgh · Cambridge · Durham · USA

First published in 2000 by
The Pentland Press Ltd.
1 Hutton Close
South Church
Bishop Auckland
Durham

British Library Cataloguing in Publication Data.
A catalogue record for this book is available
from the British Library.

ISBN 1 85821 761 X

Typeset by George Wishart & Associates, Whitley Bay.
Printed and bound by Bookcraft (Bath) Ltd.

The Author, 1945.

Contents

Illustrations and Maps

Foreword

My reasons for publishing this book taken from my privately printed memoirs are set out in the Introduction.

Here I wish to thank those that helped me. My old friend Sir Ludovic Kennedy, the author and broadcaster, who very kindly read and corrected the proofs, as has General Sir Michael Gow, a fellow, but younger, officer in the 3rd Battalion Scots Guards. I am grateful for his advice on matters affecting the Regiment. During my research, the staff at the Public Record Office guided me patiently through their computer systems, and those at the library of the Imperial War Museum were equally helpful.

Regimental Headquarters Scots Guards put their archives at my disposal and John Peaty of the British Commission for Military History allowed me to quote from his 1997 lecture.

The editor of the *Spectator* agreed to the inclusion of Bruce Anderson's article of 31 May 1997, which occasioned the publishing, in due course, of this book.

I am also grateful to Major General Peter Leuchars, formerly Welsh Guards, who made available material on the fighting at Chêndollé in Normandy.

Finally I must thank my friend John Grigg, the President

of the London Library, for encouraging me to go into print.

I hope that my friends in the Squadron and the Battalion (sadly there are not too many of them still with us) will accept my portrayal of our times together. However, in war every man sees the action from his own perspective, I can only put down my own.

Introduction

This book stems from a memoir of my life written over the last two or three years which is to be printed privately for my family.

As I wrote the war chapters, based partly on notes made shortly after the War and on reading of post-war histories, I came to feel out of sympathy with much of the revisionist views which have come to be widely accepted.

I disagree in particular with the low assessment of the fighting quality of the Allied military forces as compared to that of the German Army in the Normandy Campaign in 1944, and in the subsequent campaign in North-West Europe up to the Germans' final surrender in 1945.

The phrase used to describe the British and Canadian armies in Normandy by some writers is the 'flawed instrument in the hands of their Commander-in-Chief', Montgomery. The general basis of their assessment is that the fighting quality of the British and Canadian units in 21st Army Group was such that they were unable to make any progress in attacks against the German forces without overwhelming air and artillery support, due to the higher fighting quality of the German soldiers.

This view has been to some degree encouraged by the national natural inclination towards understatement of many British participants – a very typical reaction from the officer class to which most of the writers and contributors belong. A reaction which is not shared by their former enemies, to judge from the relatively sparse German material that is generally available.

The views which I express in this book grew primarily from my experiences as a major in the 3rd Battalion Scots Guards, commanding a Churchill Tank Squadron, the Battalion forming part of 6th Guards Tank (later armoured) Brigade.

I took command of the Squadron at the end of July 1944 when Willie Whitelaw, the then commander, was promoted to be Battalion Second in Command, after Sydney Cuthbert was killed in action in the first day's fighting. I had previously landed on D-Day as an observer for 6th Guards Tank Brigade and after reporting back my experiences, returned in July with the Battalion to Normandy.

During the campaign up to the Baltic coast in the following year, my Squadron fought closely in support of a range of British Infantry Regiments and on occasion with United States and Canadian units.

As I read the post-war literature, not least the German material, I came to the conclusion that the fighting quality of the British, Canadian and American units had been seriously understated and the performance of the Germany Army overrated. There were, of course, great differences in the quality of the troops within both the opposing armies, but this variation from the excellent to the indifferent was, in my view, found in much the same proportion on both sides.

What was not found on the Allied side was an organization for war to match the Germans. Despite clear indication of German aggressive intent since 1937 or earlier, and after nearly five years of war, our troops in Normandy in 1944 were sent into battle with inferior personal automatic weapons, inferior mortars, inferior close anti-tank weapons, and seriously under-gunned tanks. It was only in artillery that the British and Americans were a match for the Germans and, of course, in the air our supremacy was virtually complete, but in my experience the advantage was seldom made use of at the point of battle. In the only close interventions by the RAF or USAF which we experienced, we were in fact the target.

On a wider front, the Army had been poorly served, not just by a poor choice and development of weaponry, but by training in the early years of the War, based largely on First World War experience. It took far too long to assimilate the lessons of the German Blitzkrieg in Poland in 1939 and France in 1940. It was not, for example, until near the end of the Normandy campaign in 1944, that the British Armoured Divisions adopted the 'Battle Group' technique pioneered and perfected in the German Army.

To add to these factors, the organization of the British Army was hide-bound and 'tail-heavy'; it is estimated that whereas in the Germany Army it took some twenty men to put one man into the front line, in the British Army it took forty-five, the American Army being even worse, taking some sixty men to put one soldier into the front line.

Fortunately for the Allies, the Germans had deep political and military problems, stemming largely from

Hitler's personal interventions,* and this, combined with our eventual industrial supremacy, greater manpower and the steadfastness of our fighting men, enabled the Allies to triumph.

The culminating reason which persuaded me to bring up to date and publish my memoirs of the War years was the article by Bruce Anderson in the *Spectator* of 31 May 1997†. In the article he argues that the British soldier in Normandy and Italy performed poorly, and would have performed better had the death penalty been in place and when they did their duty, it was due in fact to their fear of their NCOs.

This, as I replied in my letter to the *Spectator*, is ridiculous and offensive – and I am surprised at my restraint at the time. It is a monstrous slur and many accounts, some of them written lately, have shown how hard and successfully the Allied infantry soldiers fought right up to the time when they knew the War was very close to the end and the instinct for self-preservation was for most people at its strongest.

The fact is that in the German Army they did have the death penalty and it is reported that 4,000 were executed in the last months of the War. A deserter from a British Infantry Battalion (it was difficult to desert from an armoured vehicle!) suffered no worse a fate than to be returned to his unit and when there was a genuine

---

*David Fraser in his masterly biography *Alanbrooke* quotes Alanbrooke's remark that Hitler had been 'worth forty Divisions' to the Allied cause.
†Bruce Anderson's article and my reply are reproduced with the permission of the editor of the *Spectator* in Appendix I, p. 149.

breakdown of morale the man was sent back to the rear echelons.

The framework of this book is my experience in the Army from 1939 to 1945 and in particular in the campaign in North-West Europe. It will pay tribute to the front-line soldiers in the British, Canadian and American armies, but above all to the infantry who maintained their resolute steadfastness despite heavy and continuing casualties and in the face of many difficulties, not all caused by their enemies.

It may help to put the years I describe into context if I outline briefly how I became, somewhat surprisingly, in 1937, at the age of eighteen, a University Candidate at Christ Church, Oxford for a regular commission in the Scots Guards.

I was born in Montreal, Canada on 10 February 1919. My father, Gerald Farrell, a Montreal businessman, had returned to Canada, after education at Ampleforth College in Yorkshire, and after service as a young officer in the Boer War.

He had a successful business career in Montreal and London, at one time taking over Beaverbrook's interests in Canada, when the latter moved to England. Sadly my father died at the age of forty in 1919, when I was only a few months old.

At the age of three I left Canada when my mother took me and my three older brothers to England to be educated at Ampleforth, as my father had wished, and where he had been the outstanding athlete of his generation.

When I was thirteen my three older brothers, having

finished their schooling, my mother and they decided to return to Canada and for my brothers to go to McGill University in Montreal. My mother offered me the choice of continuing my education at Ampleforth (or Dartmouth which I was very keen to go to) or of returning to Canada with them.

I chose to stay in England which was the only country I knew, and loved. My guardian became Marion Minto, a niece and a very close friend of my mother's, who had married a border peer, Larry Minto.

Minto became my home, and a very happy one, for the Christmas and Easter holidays. I would usually return to Canada for the summer holiday to be with my mother and brothers.

I took the entry examination for Dartmouth and after having passed the interview, (which was quite a daunting experience for a thirteen-year-old facing a uniformed Navy board sitting in a very grand room in Admiralty Arch) failed the medical due to my short-sight.

A year or two later Larry Minto suggested I go into his old regiment, the Scots Guards. I liked the idea and was, in due course, interviewed and accepted.

In 1937 I left Ampleforth and went to Christ Church, Oxford as a university candidate for a regular commission in the Scots Guards.

For the last year at Ampleforth I had been in the History Scholarship class with only two others, Patrick O'Donovan and Hugh Dormer, tutored by Mr Charles Edwards, a friendly and inspiring master. In 1937 Hugh, Patrick and I went up together to Christ Church, they having won exhibitions and I not having taken the scholarship examination due to my mother's opposition. She believed, as did many of her generation, that scholarships should be left to those whose families could ill-afford the fees.

It is from this time at Christ Church in 1938 that the memoirs begin.

CHAPTER 1

Spring 1938 to September 1939

In the spring of 1938 Hugh Dormer and I set off on a walking tour of Bavaria after our first two terms at Christ Church, Oxford following Ampleforth, where he had been head of the School and I head of my house, under two outstanding men Father Paul Nevill, the headmaster and Father Stephen Marwood, my housemaster. We were struck by the beauty of the country, the monasteries, rococo churches and Mad King Ludwig's palace. We found that we were greeted with friendliness by the farmers on our route down to Murnau, who would offer us a glass of milk or beer as we stopped by their houses. However, the overwhelming sense was of a nation bent on war. Not a day passed without seeing marching columns of men singing Nazi anthems, whether soldiers or schoolchildren. Even the labour corps, the agricultural workers, with their shovels or picks carried on their shoulders like rifles marched with military precision.

At the end of the walking tour we arrived in Nuremberg where Hugh's uncle, George Ogilvy-Forbes, the Minister at the British Embassy in Berlin, had provided us with tickets for seats in the diplomatic enclosure at the annual Party

Rally, the great Nazi festival of the year, attended by Hitler and all the leaders of the Nazi Party. The town was packed with troops – SS officers and men in their black uniforms, storm troopers in brown – and a vast influx of ordinary spectators in what was an atmosphere of high holiday and celebration.

There were no restrictions on movement, nor any obvious security precautions. On more than one occasion we saw the top members of the party – Goering, Hess, Goebbels and the rest – walking in the street or eating in the same restaurants as ourselves. There was more formality at the opera where we got seats for a performance of *Gotterdämmerung*, attended by Hermann Goering. He was greeted with a mass singing by the full cast and the audience of the Horst Wessel song, followed by 'Deutschland Uber Alles', both at the beginning and end of the performance. The atmosphere was so oppressive and the association of Wagner with the Nazi Party so strong that since then I have never taken the initiative to go to any performance of his work. During the day we wandered in the town watching the military parades and visiting the various exhibitions, mainly glorifying the Nordic race in paintings and photographs.

We came across one particularly distasteful exhibition which continued the Nordic cult while showing a series of offensive and obscene anti-Christian exhibits linking Christianity with Judaism.

The great event was the parade in the main stadium each evening, climaxed by a speech by the Führer. The atmosphere here was one of unmistakable war hysteria. The chant of '*Sieg Heil*' burst from the audience at every opportunity. Albert Speer had constructed the setting for these events, and in the evening he had arranged for a continuous ring of searchlights around the stadium so that as darkness fell a wall of light was created in a complete circle, the famous 'cathedral of light', as it was inappropriately called. In preparation for Hitler's speech, the loudest cheer would go up for the black-uniformed SS regiment who maintained the goose step for the longest distance after passing the saluting base on which Hitler stood.

Hitler's speech began quietly and ended by working the vast crowd up to a fever pitch of excitement. No-one hearing him and hearing the reaction could doubt that here was a nation in the grip of a leadership hell-bent on aggressive war. Hugh and I had no doubt of this. We had decided that while we would stand for their national anthem we would remain seated during the playing of the Host Wessel song, the Nazi anthem which always followed 'Deutschland Uber Alles'. There was considerable hostility to us, even in the diplomatic stand, and I am sure it was only diplomatic protocol which saved us from an attack by the police or members of the audience. We were content to have made our small protest.

Hugh was to win the DSO working for SOE with the Resistance in France in 1943. He personally organized the destruction of a Shale oil plant in the south-west, having reconnoitred it under the noses of the German guards, planted the explosives and organized the safe withdrawal of his group. There can have been no question of him posing, if questioned, as a Frenchman, as his accent was positively Churchillian. He returned to his regiment, the Irish Guards, to go with them to Normandy in 1944 only to be killed in their advance south of Caumont.

It was an eerie situation to return to England and to Oxford in the summer of 1938 and to hear so many, particularly those of the previous generation, speaking out against re-armament and in favour of appeasement, but then we had not experienced at first hand the horrors of the First World War which had only ended twenty years before. I was certain in my mind that there could not be many months of peace left to us, but I had not reckoned with Neville Chamberlain and his 'Peace with Honour'.

The news of this came to me as I was returning from the summer vacation which I spent with my family in Canada, the last time I was to see them for seven years. On hearing the news alone in my cabin over the loudspeaker system I was overwhelmed with the shame of it.

There is a wide variety of argument as to whether the year's grace which we gained was to our advantage. My feeling is that the Nazi re-armament was much faster than our own, and that the military gap between Germany and France and ourselves widened to our disadvantage in the period. There can be little doubt that the best moment to stop Hitler in his tracks lay with the French when he moved to re-occupy the Rhineland in 1935; unfortunately then and later the political will was lacking.

This trip to Canada in July 1938 to see my family followed immediately after my month's attachment to the First Battalion of the Scots Guards which was stationed at

Chelsea Barracks in London. This attachment was part of the preparation of a university candidate for a regular commission, and my time in the barracks was shared with Robin Whigham who was an undergraduate at Cambridge, also as a Scots Guards university entrant. He was later killed in Italy in 1945. We were dressed, at our own expense, for this single fortnight, as Second Lieutenants in the Territorial Army General List without regimental insignia.

Life was curious in that we found ourselves almost alone in the Officers' Mess during that July of 1938. Only the Duty, or Picket Officer, as he was called, went about his duties each day; the Adjutant would appear occasionally and have a friendly word but our time was mainly spent at drill on the square as part of a squad under the tuition of a drill sergeant. We stood behind the Commanding Officer at his 'Orders' when offenders of the previous week were brought before him. He came into barracks to take these in his London suit, and to dispense justice against a background of shouted commands and crashing heels. One case which sticks in my mind was of a sergeant who was charged with molesting a drummer boy in his barrack room during the night. At the end of the evidence the Commanding Officer asked the boy, 'Did you scream or cry out?' On being told 'no' the Commanding Officer said briefly, 'Case dismissed'.

Robin and I spent much of our time quietly reading in the Officers' Mess between drill parades and wondering if the door would ever open. We were both amazed at the Olympian calm and utter military inactivity. We told ourselves that this was no doubt a summer holiday period, and why should most of the officers not be on leave? Nevertheless, it crossed my mind that the SS regiments I had seen goose-stepping in the stadium at Nuremberg that spring were unlikely to be in a state of summer torpor, but rather on manoeuvres close to the Czech border.

We learnt to drill and, when out of uniform, to wear a dark suit, sober silk tie and shirt, stiff white collar, carry an umbrella, pigskin gloves and wear a bowler hat. More seriously, we also began to realize something of the great strength given to the Regiment by the senior Non-Commissioned Officers and Warrant Officers in whose charge we mainly were. However, the worry of that torpor in the summer of 1938 remains with me. It was the first of many instances of 'the powers that be' failing to make the British Army, even at that late date, into the professional, highly trained body which it deserved and needed to be, and which it eventually, through many disasters, became, although always under equipped in comparison to the German Army.

On leaving Chelsea Barracks I sailed for Quebec on the *Empress of Britain*, a new luxury liner and the pride of the Canadian Pacific fleet. The ship was of 42,000 tonnes and the only one ever to have a full-sized tennis court on its top deck; it was sunk by German aircraft in the Irish Sea three years later. My mother always sent me the ticket for the voyage, and on this occasion she put me in cabin, not first class. On discovering that Robin Whigham was travelling on holiday with his mother and father, and his brother and sister, in first class I paid the difference myself in order to travel with them.

I did not regret the expenditure, mainly due to the presence of a stunning American girl from Wellesley College who was crossing with her parents, an American Admiral and his wife. I took every opportunity to spend time with her, and when on the last night we kissed for the first time on the boat deck, I can still remember the shock of utter pleasure and near blackout of delight of a very innocent nineteen-year-old. My last memories of her are of being invited unusually by her family to take breakfast with them at their table on the last morning, and standing pressed close to her side on the fortunately crowded rail to watch the ship dock at Quebec. All our plans to meet in the USA during my six weeks' holiday in Montreal came to nought, mainly due to my mother's gentle but firm non-cooperation. I was not to see her again.

I returned, with some surprise, to Christ Church, having anticipated the outbreak of war, to what was to have been my second but which turned out also to be my last year at Oxford. The year was one of considerable academic idleness, balanced by an active social life and travel abroad. The only steady attendance during the term was at the Senior Officer Training Corps meetings and parades. I had joined the Cavalry section of the Corps, and although I was awarded my certificate 'B' I have no memory of learning anything that was even remotely militarily useful – a balance I attempted to alter by steady reading of Clausewitz and Foch and I still have the copious notes I made at the time.

On the day war was declared, September 3rd, I listened to Neville Chamberlain's broadcast with some friends in a flat overlooking South Kensington tube station and heard the declaration of war with relief, as I and many others had the feeling, not without reason, that Chamberlain would find some means of evading our country's treaty obligations and, in my view, our own national interest. Minutes after the declaration of war, air-raid sirens sounded and we watched people running to take shelter in South Kensington tube station as they were to do with good reason the following year.

The end of an era was at hand, and the changes of life in England which the Second World War was to bring were far greater than those of the First World War. I was fortunate to have seen and enjoyed the pre-war life of a perhaps overindulged undergraduate. My main regret is that I did not take more advantage of the academic opportunities of those two years at Oxford when so much learning was there to be taken so easily.

The extent of the officer casualties in the Second World War is not always appreciated. At Christ Church, the Roll of Honour of members of 'The House' who were killed in the two wars was of a similar order, the Roll of Honour for the First World War being 226, and for the Second World War 206. At Ampleforth, the Roll of Honour of those killed in the First World War was 84, and in the Second World War 127. In the Scots Guards, 111 officers were killed in the First World War and 98 in the Second. Other rank casualties were, however, far greater in the First World War – as an indicator, in the Scots Guards 943 other ranks were killed in the Second World War against 2,730 in the First. I have never seen any reasoned explanation why the officers ratio of casualties in the Scots Guards was so high in the Second World War, 9.4 per cent of the total in the Second World War against 3.8 per cent in the First World War. The overall statistics of the breakdown of casualties between officers and other ranks in the Second World War are curiously not yet available.

But in October 1939 all this lay in the future. The confirmation of my appointment as a Second Lieutenant, or Ensign as it was known in the Scots Guards, arrived from Regimental Headquarters, with instructions as to uniform and the information that my reporting instructions would follow. I set off on a round of visits to fit myself out appropriately with service dress, blue evening uniform and blue-grey greatcoat, Sam Browne belt (and a sword, never to be worn), shoes and boots, khaki cap and blue and gold-trimmed forage cap, regulation mackintosh and the rest.

All fitted out I waited for orders to report. For the three week interval I divided my time between Minto and Mellerstain, the home of Marion's sister Sarah who had followed in her footsteps and married a neighbouring Border Peer, Geordie Haddington. They were very kind to me and as Sarah was in London I found myself alone at Mellerstain with Geordie and a very beautiful guest who cheered up those waiting weeks and who I used to take punting on the lake at Mellerstain. I have a memory of her looking at me with a rather amused and perhaps speculative eye. However all my attention was devoted to the arrival of the post each morning.

Eventually, in the middle of October, I received the order to attend at the Scots Guards Training Battalion in Pirbright Camp, and I set off in my new uniform for my destination full of pride and trepidation.

CHAPTER II

October 1939 to D-Day 1944

Life in the Scots Guards Training Battalion was very strange to a newly joined officer, but was lived against a background of the arrival of others of the same age, some of whom were to follow the same path through the Regiment. In the six years I served until 1945, I continued to be both proud and happy in the Scots Guards, and those I served with are those of my friends I am always happiest to see again, no matter how long the interval of time may be.

Life was centred around 'drills on the square', and the immediate ambition was to 'pass off'. There was a combination of being treated like a raw recruit by the senior Warrant Officers who took the drill squads, and then to go back to a private room in the barracks to find fresh uniform laid out and a bath run by the soldier servant (as he was known in those days) who was allotted to each officer with no other duties except to 'valet' that officer and make sure he appeared neat and correctly dressed at all times. An officer in the Brigade of Guards was always well looked after.

Looking ahead as a Major commanding a tank squadron in Europe in the campaign in 1944–45, apart from my own tank and crew, I had for my personal use a Daimler armoured scout car with driver, a jeep with driver, a Humber staff car with driver (a special vehicle allocated squadrons in a tank battalion as they so often operated independently), and lastly my personal soldier servant. The contrast with the much leaner resources in manpower and vehicles allotted to an equivalent commander in a German panzer division was considerable. But, more importantly, the German commander's tanks were better gunned, better armoured and generally better designed. There was, I think, no British tank commander who would not happily have surrendered his 'fringe benefits' for a tank in the same class as the German Panther or Tiger. My soldier servant's only other duty was to act as co-driver in the squadron water truck, which also brought up the mail and, more importantly, the cigarette rations. The attitude to smoking was very different in those days. Almost without exception officers and men smoked, and smoked heavily. Smoking in the tanks was officially not allowed, but once in battle all tank crew members smoked during any pause in the action. A serious blow to morale was any mishap to the water truck, not so much because of the mail or the water, but because it carried the cigarette rations.

To return to Pirbright after eventually passing off the square, some afternoons were spent learning the intricacies of the Scottish reel in the gymnasium. Luckily, I was well prepared for this by the long succession of parties and dances for the young that I had attended in the Borders at Minto in my teens – not long past. I was twenty when I joined at Pirbright.

Passing off the square was a considerable relief. The Regimental Sergeant Major, Freddie Archer, who often himself took the young officers' squad, would, when after some weeks the desired standard had been reached, leave us with the words, 'Remember, march proud, Sir, march proud, as though you own the ground you walk on.'

There was a relaxed talk by the Adjutant in the vein that nothing he said would, of course, be new to us, but he would mention that 'London was 'visited', and the phrase 'going up to town' never used, and that a play or musical was never to be referred to as 'a show'. Spirits or sherry, when taken, were always to be 'a glass of . . .', never 'a sherry' or 'a whisky'. Dress was easy as we were usually in uniform, but we were reminded that we were always, in London, to wear gloves and carry a stick – ash, in the case of the Scots Guards – and that a parcel was never to be carried. If by chance we were in London in plain clothes, heaven forbid that this should be referred to as 'mufti'. We were to wear a dark suit, black shoes, stiff white collar with a discreet silk tie and sober shirt, and when outdoors to wear a bowler hat and carry gloves and an umbrella which should never be unfurled unless to protect a lady from the rain. The memory of this brings a smile, but it was all part of the induction of high standards in the young officer.

Our military training was based on First World War experience, and further circumscribed by a shortage of automatic weapons, even of the long-outdated Lewis gun. The training was in the hands of officers who had fought in the First World War and who assumed that the Second World War would follow the same pattern. The German blitzkrieg through Poland had shown a few months before, how outdated our military thinking was. Much of our time was spent in the construction of a large trench system with its accompanying dugouts which, when completed, formed the basis of our day and night exercises. A particular memory is of the youngest officers being sent out to lead night patrols while 'the old', as we thought of them, remained in the Officers' Mess dugout which was well supplied with port and whisky. One Major, in a fit of absence of mind, and to everyone's delight, had his trench system dug facing in the wrong direction, and his fortification was known for many years afterwards as 'Victor's Folly'.

We were, at the same time, more usefully absorbing the traditions and history of the Regiment, to such simple and fundamental rules that the welfare of the men must always come before that of the officers – on every occasion no officer should consider his own needs until he was sure that his men were fully provided for. We were thus absorbing lessons of officer behaviour and discipline, but that was all. The training, except in the use of small arms and patrolling, had little to do with the Second World War.

The winter passed agreeably enough in good company with enjoyable visits to London, but frustratingly in the time of the 'phoney war'. The Regiment had one service battalion in England, and the second in Egypt, but the chance of being sent to either was, at this stage, remote.

In February 1940, an opportunity to escape to something more interesting presented itself. The Russian invasion of Finland, following on their pact with the Nazis and their joint invasion of Poland the previous September, shocked the free world. An expedition force, at four to five divisions in strength, mounted by the French and British governments, was planned to land in Norway at Narvik, cross northern Sweden, thus neutralizing their valuable iron-ore resources, and thence to Finland in support of the Finns in their hard-pressed struggle, and who, despite their vastly inferior numbers, were succeeding in holding their own.

It was considered vital that this force should have a ski battalion for its forward patrols and to this end an appeal went out throughout the Army, and beyond, for anyone who had good knowledge of skiing to volunteer for service with such a battalion. This was to be known as the Fifth (SR) Battalion Scots Guards under the command of a Coldstream Officer, Jimmy Coats, and with a Scots Guards Adjutant, Digby Raeburn. Officers volunteering were asked to resign their commissions and to serve in the ranks for the period of the campaign, after which their commissions and seniority would be restored. Over one thousand men volunteered from all walks of life, and eventually, after a weeding-out process, 167 Officers, 180 volunteers from civilian life, and 73 Officer Cadets were chosen, and this 420 was supplemented by one company of regular Scots Guardsmen from the 1st Battalion under their Company Commander, Dick Gurowski.

To the obvious irritation of our Commanding Officer at Pirbright, Colonel Alan Swinton, three officers – David Stirling, Andrew Maxwell and I – all volunteered and were accepted. During February a motley crew of recruits assembled at Bordon in Hampshire under the amazed eyes of officers and warrant officers of the First Battalion of the Scots Guards who had been appointed to help with the organization of the new ski battalion. We were then equipped with the new Mark IV Lee-Enfield rifle and Arctic clothing, but with no automatic weapons or mortars. Battalion HQ even had no wireless. In the first week of March, the Battalion set off for a secret destination, which rumours placed widely between the Arctic and the Mediterranean, but which turned out to be Chamonix, for training by the Chasseur Alpin. One of the surprises of the move was the sheer weight of the pack to be carried – over 100 lb – quite a contrast to the well-ordered life of a Pirbright officer with his soldier servant.

On arrival at Chamonix, we found ourselves comfortably billeted in the local hotels, and as there seemed to be few qualified cooks among us we were allowed to use the resources of the hotels and ate well. The training was not intensive because the local Chasseur Alpin told us that there was too great an avalanche danger to allow us to go high up the slopes by cable car. They put on a few demonstrations on the lower slopes, and there was, despite the warnings, some enjoyable skiing on the upper slopes. Practical loading and unloading of sledges took place under the eyes of two Polar explorers we had with us – Gino Watkins and Martin Lindsay.

The company of regular guardsmen delighted in their unexpected holiday, and within days were skiing down the slopes without fear and with some skill.

It was a curious sensation to be dressed as a guardsman,

having been very proud to be an officer in the Scots Guards, but the intense frustration of the phoney war and its air of unreality made this 'escapade' well worthwhile to a young man about to celebrate his 21st birthday. Had the expedition carried out its objectives and landed in Norway, crossed northern Sweden, arrived in Finland and joined battle with the Russians, I expect that the majority of my fellow guardsmen (as the ski forward patrols of such a force) might have started to take a different view. The odds on survival of even a small minority would have been slight.

The expedition was, with hindsight, ill-conceived, both politically and militarily, and had the high professionalism which later developed been in place at the time, it would not have been given a second thought; and I suspect that the operational planner who produced it returned to duty with his regiment. The official history throws little light on why the British and French authorities mounted such an expedition – massively ill-equipped – to land in north Norway without the Norwegian Government's agreement, to cross into Sweden without the Swedish Government's agreement, in order to neutralize the Swedish iron-ore works at Gallevans, on their way into Finland, and finally to go to war with the Soviet Empire. Anyone interested in exploring ill-conceived military/ political initiatives should have a field day with this aborted campaign. It remains a mystery how it came to be approved by the Cabinet and the Chiefs of Staff.

After two weeks, orders came for our urgent return to England, and our departure from Chamonix was reported very accurately on the German radio. As we travelled across France, under what was intended to be conditions of great secrecy, the sight of the Buffet de la Gare at Dijon proved too much for the independently-minded ex-officers who poured out of the train and occupied the buffet. A happy memory is of Digby Raeburn, the Adjutant, standing with outstretched arms attempting to stem the tide, but to no avail.

The Battalion finally reached the Clyde and embarked on a Polish ship, the *Batory*, where we were taught by the sailors how to sling our hammocks. After two days, and just before we set sail, the Finns made peace with the Russians. The expedition was stood down, the Battalion returned to Bordon, we officers received our commissions back and returned to our regiments – in the case of David Stirling, Andrew Maxwell and myself somewhat ingloriously to the Training Battalion at Pirbright. David and Andrew both shortly afterwards escaped again to the more exciting and individual world of the irregular soldier. I volunteered for most opportunities which arose – commandos, parachutists, etc. – but was routinely refused. Perhaps if I had pushed harder I might have succeeded, but as the years went by I felt myself happily more and more part of the regimental community of the Scots Guards and in particular of the, in our view, rather exceptionally officered Third Battalion which I eventually joined.

There was another factor: front-line soldiers, and above all the infantry were the vital element in any fighting force. Their role was the hardest. Infantry casualties were double or more those in the more specialist arms of tanks, gunners or engineers, and four or five times those in the support echelons of a field force. Even these figures do not adequately reflect the leading role played in battle by the front-line infantryman; to be in a rifle company was one thing, but to be, say, at Battalion HQ or in a Battalion transport echelon, was quite another. The casualties in the infantry were of an order which drained the manpower of this country, so that by the time of the Normandy fighting the Army had reached the limit of its resources, after which manpower gradually declined to the point that the casualties could not be replaced.

The problems of those in command of our higher formations were in consequence acute, but the real stress fell on the infantry battalions. In the light of this grave manpower crisis which was, by 1944, causing brigades and divisions to be 'melted down', it was astonishing that we did not succeed in reducing our back-up forces so that they, at least, approached the German level. Another factor was our vast anti-aircraft command, perhaps justifiable in the early 1940s, but as we gradually achieved complete air supremacy in Europe by 1943/44 it could have been slashed in order to provide infantry reinforcements, or, as mentioned in a later chapter, at least used as anti-tank units in a ground role with their high velocity 3.7" guns which would have matched the German 88s.

John Peaty in a study presented to the British Commission for Military History in 1998 pointed out that an additional factor which drained the resources available to the infantry was the existence of the private armies, as he described them, which absorbed the manpower equivalent to ten infantry divisions. He refers to such special forces as four 'commando' brigades, two airborne divisions, one parachute brigade, one mountain division, six 'Chindit' brigades, one Polish parachute brigade and one Indian parachute brigade. John Peaty goes on to say that three things are clear. Firstly that a large quantity of high-quality manpower was diverted away from the infantry and into special forces (used in the widest sense) during the War. Secondly that measured by time spent in contact with the enemy or by damage inflicted on the enemy, special forces did not repay the heavy investment made in them. Thirdly that this division of manpower into special forces and away from the infantry helped to cause and exacerbate the infantry shortage which afflicted the British Army in the latter part of the War.

He cites as one of the worst offenders the Airborne Forces – given the infantry shortage, it is hard to justify the deployment in NW Europe of two airborne divisions, one of whom saw action for just nine days, instead of two additional infantry divisions.

Peaty's judgement is perhaps too harsh in these instances, as those he refers to were trained fighting formations, although too seldom used. In particular the gallantry and professionalism of the Airborne forces on D-Day, at Arnhem and at the Rhine crossing was self-evidently beyond praise.

The existence of the equivalent of ten divisions of manpower locked up in the anti-aircraft command and the long administrative tail of the Allied force remains much more difficult to explain as was our failure to deploy our airborne troops in a normal infantry role, when not actively engaged in air operations, as was the normal practice in the German Army.

The extent to which the professional classes in the United Kingdom, as perhaps in no other country, provided the main source of officer recruitment for the fighting regiments of the British Army has been little recognised. In the Scots Guards, and no doubt in many other regiments, the rate of officer casualty against other ranks was twice as high as in the First World War as I refer to earlier.

Tower of London

On my return from the ski battalion I was posted, in the spring of 1940, to the Tower of London where the holding battalion of the Scots Guards was stationed and where reinforcement drafts and officers were posted prior to being sent to service battalions. Because of the Blitz which followed, and the strong and delightful personality of our Commanding Officer, Eric MacKenzie, the spirit of an Active Service Battalion was, to a great extent, created.

As the position in France during the summer grew worse, our spirits, along with those of so many others in the country, rose to the challenge. On 8 June we heard that four officers were to go to the beaches at Dunkirk to assist in the evacuation; the Commanding Officer was pestered with applications. To the disappointment of the younger members of the Battalion, he chose what we regarded as three old officers in their thirties – to join him. They did by all accounts all that was required of them, and one, Captain Dick Gurowski, who had been with us at

Chamonix, was killed when his ship was hit by a bomb on the return voyage.

Many years later, in the 1960s, when I was Managing Director of British Sidac, a business colleague of mine, Lloyd Robinson (Chairman of the Dickinson Robinson Group) told me of a 'Dunkirk' incident which had stuck indelibly in his memory. In June 1940, as a young officer in the Warwickshire Regiment, he was sent temporarily to be the Railway Transport Officer at Leamington Spa with the job of meeting the trains bringing back survivors from Dunkirk and billeting them in the town or in the military camp beyond it.

On one train which pulled in to the platform on which he stood, there was the usual gradual emptying of the carriages onto the platform of individual soldiers and groups, tired, bedraggled and battle-worn, men and officers, a few with their equipment, but mainly without rifles or steel helmets and none in organized units.

Lloyd Robinson noticed the end carriage of the train remained closed and as he walked up to it, he met a Subaltern and an Ensign in the Welsh Guards who asked him if it was their final destination. On hearing it was the senior of the two told the Sergeant Major to get everyone out of the train onto the platform. Some 40–50 men got out, although equally battle-worn, tired and bedraggled, nearly all with their rifles and helmets, and formed up in two ranks as on parade and when they were stood at ease, the Subaltern asked for further orders. Lloyd Robinson explained the arrangements were for the men to be 'bussed' to a camp on the far side of the town and the officers to be billeted in the town. The Subaltern replied, 'I don't think you realise that we are No. 3 Company of the First Battalion of the Welsh Guards and there can be no question of splitting up the officers and men.' Lloyd Robinson immediately agreed and said that if they would get in the buses waiting for them, they would all be taken to the camp together.

The Subaltern then asked him, 'How far is this camp?' and on being told it was about a mile the far side of the town, said they would prefer to march – and march they did, very smartly, headed by their two officers, right through the centre of Leamington Spa and to the camp beyond. At the entrance to the camp, the Commandant, a Colonel of the First World War, had been warned by Lloyd Robinson what had happened. As they marched in, he turned the guard out to salute them and stood himself at the salute with tears running down his face. This story perhaps tells as much about the Brigade of Guards as do the many more stirring accounts of their gallantry in action.

Back in the Tower of London, invasion was now felt to be imminent, and we young officers welcomed the thought that the Germans would attempt it and were certain of their failure. The Battalion at the Tower of London was given part of the inner ring of London defence as a sector. My first command was that of the 'Assault Platoon' – four very small ex-Selfridge's vans into each of which we crammed six large guardsmen with their rifles, petrol bombs and, our pride and joy, slabs of gelignite, primers and detonators. The plan was that we would ambush and blow off the tracks of the German tanks with our explosives, and then drop our 'Molotov cocktails' down their turrets. We practiced in Epping Forest and in parts of the East End which had been bombed.

It is easy now to smile at the recollection of the flimsy little vans and the large guardsmen, but looking back with the hindsight of a tank commander, I would not have liked to have met such a group of trained and determined soldiers in close country or in a built-up area. When we got to Germany in February 1945, the German Army – except in certain limited instances – did not put up anything like the fierce resistance that I am sure they would have met in England in 1940 had they invaded. There are obviously many reasons for this, but that is the fact of the matter as regards their resistance in the West.

When the London Blitz started on 7 September 1940, the view from the Tower, and in particular from the top of the White Tower, was unrivalled, and that afternoon we saw for the first time what we had always imagined and seen in many films – squadron after squadron of German bombers, in formation, flying steadily over London, dropping bombs at will, although on this first and only large-scale daylight raid, the targets were nearly all in the East End and dock areas.

We did not realize at the time that Hitler, by switching his bombers from their attacks on our fighter airfields which were stretched to their limits and with a dwindling reserve of pilots, was losing probably his last chance of knocking England out of the War. Had he continued with the airfield attacks, followed by parachute drops, he might have created conditions which would have made a sea invasion possible and put the outcome of the War in a new perspective.

In writing this I feel the almost palpable disapproval and disagreement of the naval friends of my generation. To one of these, Ludovic Kennedy, I am indebted for reminding me of the words of Lord St Vincent to the House of Lords as Napoleon's Grande Armée was massed on the Channel coast. He told the House, 'I do not say they cannot come, my Lords, I only say they cannot come by sea.'

None of this, however, crossed the minds of the group of young officers gathered at the top of the White Tower, the highest point of the Tower of London, on the evening of 7 September 1940 watching the extraordinary sight of what appeared to be a sea of flames engulfing the whole of the dock area and the East End of London, fed by a continuing stream of German bombers. The Tower of London was hit by high-explosive bombs thirteen times during the Blitz (some of them luckily fell in the moat) and by very many more incendiaries. Late on another September night one bomb demolished the building immediately next to the Officers' Mess. At the time it was housing a certain Major Wintle (who emerged unhurt) who had been incarcerated in the Tower for having threatened an Air Vice Marshal – or so the story went – who was refusing his request to order the RAF planes under his command to make their escape to England. It is not difficult to imagine where our sympathies lay. Major Wintle was always accompanied by one young officer as he took his daily exercise on the battlements of the Tower; and he always worked a small rubber ball in his right hand in order, so he told us, to strengthen the muscles in his arm for polo.

In his book *The Secret War*, Professor R.V. Jones gives a somewhat different account of the events which led up to Wintle being put under close arrest. The version I have given was certainly believed by the officers guarding him at the Tower. He was a delightful man who reminisced happily as we walked along the battlements. Major Wintle suffered only a severe reprimand at his court martial and was later dropped into France by SOE, captured, imprisoned in Toulon and escaped to Spain. He was in the news again after the War when he visited the offices of a solicitor whom he believed was tricking a relative out of money, and removed the man's trousers. He was summoned for assault, went to prison, and on coming out succeeded in proving his case against the solicitor. A true and delightful eccentric.

The Battalion, whilst maintaining its anti-invasion role, had the immediate task of 'support of the civil power' as the battalion closest to the most heavily bombed areas of the East End, the docks and the City. The task here was to assist the fire and other services which were stretched beyond all measure. Then in the morning, after the all-clear had sounded, a company would often march behind the battalion pipe band through the worst-hit areas to help morale, which at times was understandably not high.

One of the worst incidents had to be dealt with by a fellow officer at the Tower. A school had suffered a direct hit with horrendous casualties and my friend and his platoon of guardsmen spent the day helping the rescue services to recover the bodies of the dead children. There was a massive and unpublicized exodus out of the East End of London. Fortunately for national morale the public did not enjoy the unrestricted television news coverage that now accompanies any catastrophe.

On one of the early nights of the Blitz, my assault platoon was ordered to help the fire services at St Katherine's Dock, which was ablaze, only some half a mile from the Tower of London. The fire was at its height when we arrived, and the warehouses on one side of the dock were burning furiously. The fire hoses were in operation, but only on their fixed stands, with their jets of water falling uselessly into the dock itself. There was no sign of any firemen. They may well have suffered casualties before withdrawing, and it was indeed an unpleasant spot with the noise of the fire and the hoses making it impossible to hear the warning sound of a falling bomb. Our men manned the hoses and turned them unsuccessfully onto a barge which was on fire and drifting slowly across the dock to the warehouses on the only side which was not yet alight. It seemed a good opportunity for the platoon to practice its demolition skills, so I and the Platoon Sergeant with two guardsmen were about to set off in a small row-boat we had commandeered. At this moment a middle-aged civilian in a bowler hat appeared, and asked me what we were planning to do. On hearing that our intention was to sink the barge in order to prevent the fire spreading, he protested that we could not do this until he had telephoned the insurance company and obtained their permission. He disappeared, presumably to find a telephone, never to be seen again. Without waiting, we set off in our row-boat.

The high-sided barge was not easy to board, but eventually we managed it and placed our gelignite charges in the hold with a time fuse in the rather murky end of the barge which was not alight, and retreated to the dockside. As we rowed back we were rewarded with an explosion and the disappearance of the barge beneath the waters of the dock. Sadly, the warehouses which we were trying to protect were hit and set alight within the next half an hour and, as they contained jute, burnt very steadily for many weeks.

Life at the Tower of London, for a young officer, even in the Blitz, was often enjoyable. On many evenings we set off to enjoy the night life of London in our blue 'undress' uniforms and our scarlet-lined grey greatcoats. There were many girls who were equally prepared to risk the bombs and visit the night life of the capital. The Cafe de Paris, was one of the popular night spots, which was eventually bombed with heavy loss of life. In my own case, and I think that of some of my other friends, I started with an innocence which did not long survive the delightful temptations of London life in the Blitz.

At the end of each evening I would return to the Tower, back to my bedroom at the top of the Officers' Mess building where I also kept the detonators and primers under my bed for the Assault Platoon ready to hand should we be called out – a practice which did not endear me to the officer with whom I shared the room. At this point in the War, I and other young officers were almost indifferent to the dangers from bombing, and in fact the odds against becoming a casualty were great. Very gallant officers who had fought in the First World War were, with exceptions, more nervous. We were to learn later that prolonged exposure to the very much higher dangers of front-line fighting produced firstly faster reactions and, secondly with few exceptions, in the end stronger feelings of fear. There was, I think, truth in Lord Moran's saying that, in war, a man's courage is his capital, and he is always spending.

Life was certainly varied, and after Major Wintle our next visitor was a German spy under close arrest who, we were told, had been landed by rubber boat and rapidly captured. Somewhat to our surprise, orders were received that he was to be shot. The execution took place under the command of one our older First World War Officers, Philip Walters, in the miniature range one morning before breakfast. Subsequently, enemy agents who were boated or parachuted into the United Kingdom were all rounded up, and, as has been well described by J.C. Masterman, the mastermind of the process, 'turned' and used to pass fake information to Germany. The proof of the success of our deceptions, counter-intelligence and security work was outstandingly demonstrated by the complete surprise achieved in 1944 – both as to place and time. Until the breakout from Normandy at the end of July 1944, the Germans continued to believe that there might be a second major landing in the Pas de Calais area and retained their divisions there to meet it, with some effect on the early fighting in Normandy. The major credit should however go to the RAF with their destruction of the German coastal radar sites and their prevention of any air reconnaissance of the D-Day build-up in the south of England.

One of the duties of the Battalion at the Tower of London was to provide the guard mounted at Buckingham Palace and St James's Palace. This was a happy experience, as apart from the advantage of being host to one's girlfriends in the Officers' Mess at St James's Palace, any air raid warning, and they were quite frequent, was a signal for great activity.

The Guards at Buckingham Palace would run at break-neck speed from their quarters, carrying their Lewis guns, through the length of the palace corridors and up the broad flights of stairs to the roof where they would mount the guns on stands ready to engage low-flying enemy aircraft. This was not perhaps the most effective protection as a German bomber shortly afterwards demonstrated, but nevertheless was a highly enjoyable experience for the young men involved.

With a certain regret I left the Tower in October 1940 on posting to join the newly forming 3rd Battalion Scots Guards at Chigwell in Essex. This was my first appointment to a true active service battalion, having served my apprenticeship in the training and holding battalions of the Regiment – the latter, thanks to the Blitz – an unexpectedly vivid experience.

The 3rd Battalion was to be my home for the rest of the War. In it I rose from Second Lieutenant steadily, but not spectacularly, to the rank of Major at the age of twenty-four in 1944 commanding one of the three tank squadrons. In those early days in October 1940 the Battalion was in an infantry role, and its task was to defend part of the outer line of the London defence running through Epping Forest.

The Blitz in London, however, continued. It felt strange no longer to be at the centre of it and to be disturbed only by the occasional bomb far off its intended target. Our lives, though, were very much involved in building up the Battalion, and we trained hard under Lieutenant Colonel George Johnson, an exceptional soldier, whose high ability was combined with what would perhaps be called nowadays a 'laid-back' attitude to life. Had he been fired by a stronger ambition, he would, I think, undoubtedly have risen very much higher than Major General Commanding London District, from which post he eventually retired.

To my pleasure I achieved two more independent commands. Firstly, the Motorcycle Platoon, an innovation in the establishment which did not last very long, but which was a pleasant change from commanding a platoon in an infantry company. The Motorcycle Platoon Commander had, on most occasions, to travel in one of the four sidecars. From the earliest exercises I realized that the Sergeant who drove me had exceptional skills. He told me very seriously that he had learnt to drive in a circus in which his last duty, before he was recalled to the Colours, was to drive around the Wall of Death with a lion in the sidecar.

One of the devices much used by the Germans in their bombing raids at this time (October 1940) was the unexploded bomb, or UXB. It failed to explode, either because the detonator mechanism had not worked, or because it was fitted with a delayed action fuse – sometimes with an accompanying booby trap device. When the heavy bombing started in the autumn of 1940, there were only twelve Royal Engineer Officers who had trained in bomb disposal work. As casualties rose among these officers, it was decided that each battalion in or near London should send one officer for two weeks' training in bomb disposal in order to be available to back up the regular engineer officers. I was chosen for this duty from our battalion for reasons I do not know and would love to discover.

I was attached for a fortnight in late 1940 to a delightful Royal Engineer officer of Irish origin, and we responded together to calls to deal with unexploded bombs in his sector in north London. I learnt the basic technique of how to unscrew gently the detonator on the 250 lb, 500 lb or 1,000 lb bomb, usually while sitting on it, and to watch for the thin wire to show if it had been booby-trapped. My Sapper friend would, near the critical moment, casually suggest that I should take cover in a neighbouring hollow while he called out what he was doing. We had no accidents and defused a number of German bombs. Sadly he was killed – blown up a few days later after I had left him – and of the group of twelve original Sapper officers only one survived the Blitz. My skills were happily never put to the test since, with the falling-off in the intensity of the bombing in 1941, the newly trained regular Royal Engineer officers were able to cope. I have no memory of feeling any particular fear, but I must in fact at times have been terrified, were it not for the cheerful 'matter-of-factness' of my Irish friend. May he rest in peace.

On my return to the Battalion I was given a new command – the Carrier Platoon. These were small, lightly-armoured tracked vehicles designed to carry our Bren guns into action. I was delighted with the appointment and must at times have been insufferably pleased, not so much with myself, I hope, but in the role in which Fate had cast me. At the time, when talking to an older officer, John Harvey, who had a successful business career before and after the War, I told him that I did not understand how anyone could follow the profit motive in preference to serving his country. He told me, quite rightly, that he had never in his life heard such an outrageously smug remark.

Life was still interspersed with visits to London and falling in rapid succession for the charms of a variety of girls. I remember in particular one girl asking me to come to a tea dance at the Dorchester with her mother – a formidable lady, who did not, I felt, relish the attentions to her daughter of a young man with no particular prospects, financial or territorial. However, other occasions with other girls were jollier and, with some encouragement (which I recall with great affection) I gradually overcame my shyness with the opposite sex.

In 1941 a decision was made to create a Guards Armoured Division. The 3rd Battalion Scots Guards was chosen to convert to tanks, with the 4th Grenadiers and the 4th Coldstream, to form 6th Guards Armoured Brigade. We were all excited at the prospect. The Germans had shown in Poland in 1939 and in France and Belgium in 1940 what armourèd divisions could achieve in war. It was natural that the powers that be in Britain should seek to form an armoured division from among their 'elite' troops.

Although we were all enthusiastic at the time, my view now, which is shared by many others, is that the move to armour was, on balance, a mistake; not because the Guards Armoured Division and the 6th Guards Armoured Brigade (which was split off later to form an independent Tank Brigade) did not distinguish themselves in battle. They did so in no uncertain way in the campaign in North-West Europe in 1944/45. However, the effect throughout the Brigade of Guards and, indeed, the Army, would have been greater if a Guards Infantry Division had been formed, or to have had, instead, three separate Guards Infantry Brigades spread among the infantry divisions. One of the unfortunate effects of the change was to build a barrier between the 'armoured-trained' officers of the regiments and the others. There could be little cross-posting, and the effect of this was to be made worse by the long period from 1940 to 1944 when so much of the Army remained in Britain.

Another factor is that, in my experience, the infantry in the Second World War were the arbiters of the battlefield and central to success or failure. They bore the brunt of the heat and burden of the battle. The vital factor is, of course, the cooperation of all arms, but except after the breakout battle, the decision is usually achieved by resoluteness of the infantry, whether operating as part of an infantry or armoured division. I naturally speak only for the Second World War, and later developments and technology of the 'rounded' battle group and new tactics may have lessened the role of the infantry.

Finally, in the particular circumstances of the Second World War, the gradual attrition of the infantry battalion in the long years from 1939 to 1945 meant that the heaviest burden on morale was borne by the infantry in terms of strain, and certainly in terms of casualties. Martin Lindsay, in his book *So Few Came Through*, paints a very clear picture of life in the 1st Battalion Gordon Highlanders in the 51st Highland Division. The dedication of this book is one which I would echo. It is:

> To the Infantry Company Commanders – British, Canadian and American – who played a greater part than any other individuals in the liberation of Europe 1944 to 1945.

I believe that the infantry was the sole sector in which the weight of the high professionalism of the Brigade of Guards should have been deployed, and not, in the case of two brigades, in the more spectacular armoured role.

In 1941, however, we were all excited at the transformation into armour as we set out on our various courses – gunnery at Lulworth, and, in my case, to a driving and maintenance course at Bovington in Dorset. It was painfully obvious in 1941 that our tanks were few in number and antiquated in design, under-gunned and with poor mechanical reliability. We all believed that this would be corrected as the British and eventually American war machines gathered strength. Sadly time was to show that our hopes were largely to be disappointed. As far as quality was concerned the German lead in tank design lengthened as the War progressed, and we remained to the end outgunned and out-armoured. Luckily, by the time of the North-West European campaign in 1944-45, tank production in the USA had given us a very considerable numerical superiority. It is a criticism of the CIGS and the leading generals, and probably to a greater extent of Winston Churchill and the whole War Cabinet, that this question was never properly addressed. The only first-class tank that we produced, the Centurion, arrived too late to be in service during the War.

It may be that in their successful pre-occupation with the general direction of the war effort, which was indeed masterly, they allowed the detailed questions of equipment and organization in the Army to go unanswered. The priority accorded to our tank design and production was, throughout the War, unacceptably low. The whole sorry story is told in a somewhat jumbled fashion by Col Mcleod Ross in his book *The Business of Tanks 1933–1945*.

The Battalion moved to Codford St Mary on Salisbury Plain and settled down to training in its new role. One of the advantages to the officers involved in the change to armour was that we remained over the years a very close group with little interchange with the two other Scots Guards battalions. George Johnson had been promoted to command a brigade, and Hugh Kindersley came to command us. He was a splendid leader of men and I wish he could have been with us in battle, but he sadly left us in 1943 to command a glider air-landing brigade. He was badly wounded on D-Day at the very moment of linking up successfully with Shimi Lovat and his commandos from the beachhead. He was very old by our standards – in his early forties – and had won an MC as a young man in the First World War. He spent the inter-war years as a very successful merchant banker, only to return to an active fighting role when those of his contemporaries who volunteered were taking up desk or staff appointments.

The transition from armour was, in one sense, a blessing since it gave a new edge and challenge to our whole training and outlook. We settled down well in our new role hampered, unfortunately, as I have said, by poor equipment and certainly in my case by an increasing restlessness as the months and years passed. We thought we might see action in 1942, and then again in 1943, but our turn was not to come until the summer of 1944. At Codford I was promoted to Captain at the end of 1941 and became Second in Command to Willie Whitelaw in one of the three tank squadrons; for a period I was seconded as an instructor to the Guards Armoured Division Tactical School, a job which I did not particularly relish as I was conscious of my lack of battle experience. However, my solution to our tactical problems were not much disputed, probably because all the officers were as inexperienced as myself.

On my return to the Battalion I was sent for by Hugh Kindersley who told me that I had been applied for by Guards Armoured Division Headquarters to be a Staff Captain in a GSO III appointment, and that it was up to me whether I wished to accept or not. I have little memory of the incident, but wrote about it at some length to my mother in Canada. I was slightly tempted by a Staff role in a higher echelon, but decided after a little thought that I would much prefer to stay with the Battalion – a decision I never regretted.

These long years of training were made the more difficult by the constant and steady news of those of our friends in the Regiment killed in the early Desert Campaign, in North Africa, and finally in Italy.

It was, I believe, a mistake of the General Staff not to have organized a much greater exchange of officers between the Army at home and those engaged in the fighting – it would not have put too much strain on shipping or organization to have arranged such an exchange so that by D-Day in June 1944 each fighting battalion and regiment had at least three or four officers who had some months of battle experience. This combined with the very high enthusiasm and professionalism of the new units might have improved the early effectiveness in battle of the untried battalions.

One incident which occurred on Salisbury Plain, of what is now called 'friendly fire', stands out. The majority of the officers of the Guards Armoured Division were assembled to watch a demonstration of an air attack on a column of dummy transport which had been arranged in a long, convenient line on a parallel slope some half a mile away. The Hurricane fighter pilot sadly mistook the line of spectators for the line of target. As I watched the Hurricane it became clear that it was heading straight for us, and I saw the twinkling of its eight machine-guns opening fire. Everyone threw themselves to the ground, except my immediate neighbour, Patrick Stewart-Fotheringham, a keen naturalist who remained standing throughout. When

I got to my feet he was anxious to show me a beetle he was holding in his hand, of a species which he had never seen before. This unconcern for his personal safety remained with him during the rest of the War, and he won a well-deserved DSO while commanding a company in 1944. Many officers were killed or wounded in this tragic episode, which is not recorded in the official history of the Division. In those days casualties by 'friendly fire' were not the subject of publicity or litigation.

Despite the company of friends and the opportunity of fairly frequent visits to London, the round of training did not give the sort of involvement in the War in which I and my fellow officers were anxious to achieve. A small opportunity arose for me when I met at a party the Commander of the Royal Naval Motor Torpedo Boat Squadron operating out of Portsmouth.

Their role at that time was to locate and attack at night the German convoys which were creeping up and down the French coast. I asked him if I might be allowed to join them for a week, and after a little persuasion the Flotilla Commander agreed. I then had to go with some trepidation and get Hugh Kindersley's permission, which was typically given without hesitation; the following week I joined one of the MTBs at Portsmouth as a 'supernumary'. These MTBs were the fastest craft in the Royal Navy, and as we set off in the early evening darkness it was a great pleasure to be given the wheel and allowed to feel the great surge of power from the Rolls-Royce Merlin engines as I pushed the accelerator levers forward. The remainder of the experience was not so enjoyable; we lay off the French coast with our engines switched off, watching on radar for the movement of any enemy ships. I am not a good sailor, and after some nights of rocking, sick-makingly, from side to side with no enemy convoys appearing, I was happy to get back to life on Salisbury Plain.

The process of training continued with a move in 1943 to Thoresby Park in Nottinghamshire. This had been preceded by a change in role of 6th Brigade, which became the Independent 6th Guards Tank Brigade, and was re-equipped with Churchill Tanks as an independent tank formation, although for some time forming part of 15th Scottish Division. Most of us were sad to leave the Guards Armoured Division, and particularly to see our role – a false concept as it turned out – as something rather more pedestrian with close support to infantry. We were not to know that some two years later the brigade was chosen to be the leading tank formation to cross the Rhine, to join with the airborne forces and to advance some fifty miles in three days to capture Munster.

Life at Thoresby was the same round of hard training and enjoyable visits to London and Scotland; one of the more pleasurable was being best man to Willie Whitelaw at his wedding in Edinburgh in February 1943 to Celia Sprot whom I knew before the War during holidays in the Borders. Fifty years later in 1993, Willie and Celia celebrated their Golden Wedding anniversary with a large dinner party for some 200 at the National Portrait Gallery in London. As his best man, I had to propose his and Celia's health. I took trouble with my short speech as I wanted to reflect the flavour of the great affection in which

Willie and Celia were held. I was pleased when the Prime Minister John Major came up to me afterwards and said, 'That was very good, you should do it more often'.

My progress up the Battalion continued steadily, and in January 1944 a new Commanding Officer, Claude Dunbar, who had taken over from Hugh Kindersley, sent for me and told me that I was to be promoted to Major to command Left Flank Squadron as Jock Mounsey-Heysham was not in good enough health to continue. I was delighted by the promotion, I was twenty-four years of age and had achieved my immediate ambition.

The command of the Churchill Tank Squadron was a particularly favoured one. The Squadron normally operated separately from the Battalion, in support of an infantry battalion. The command was essentially an independent one in battle, which was recognised, as I have mentioned earlier, by the addition to each squadron establishment of a Humber staff car, normally not allotted lower than Battalion Commander level. I stress this because as in all that I have read about the operations of 6th Guards Tank Brigade, or indeed of the 3rd Battalion Scots Guards, this vital difference in operation from the fighting technique of a unit in the Armoured Division is not mentioned. In battle the Infantry Battalion Commander and the Tank Squadron Commander formed a tight-knit team in which the Tank Battalion Headquarters had virtually no part to play once battle was joined. This independence in battle of the individual squadron should be seen against the battalion background of a very tight-knit group of officers in the Battalion who, because of their long years of training from 1941 to 1944, had come to know each other well and, incidentally, took great pride in building up what we all believed to be an outstanding armoured formation.

Many years after the War I met General Sir Richard O'Connor at his stepson's house. O'Connor had commanded VIII Corps in Normandy, under whom we fought at Caumont, and in subsequent battles. When in reply to his question I said that I had commanded a squadron in the 3rd Battalion Scots Guards but that I did not expect him to know of it, he said that of course he had known about us and that we were the best tank formation under his command, and went on to elaborate. My already high opinion of and admiration for him grew by the minute!

The great advantage of the battalion or regimental system was that each and every member of any good battalion or regiment came to believe firmly that his unit was inarguably better than any other – and this was, of course, a great source of strength in battle, although at times tiresome to the outsider! Max Hastings in his very readable book *Overlord* criticizes the effect of the regimental system as against the wider German loyalties of the individual soldier to his Division or Corps.

I believe that the regimental or battalion unit was the best and clearest focus for an essentially citizen army and that the Scots Guards ready absorption in 1944 of large members of recruits from the RAF Regiment was a good example of the flexibility and the strength of the system.

In 1943 the Battalion moved with the Brigade to Yorkshire to what, as we always believed, would be our final training with the 15th Scottish Division before the invasion. However, 1943 slipped away with no second front. John Grigg has written interestingly and persuasively that an opportunity was missed in not mounting the invasion in 1943. In the light of what we now know of the fighting capacity of the German Army, I believe, it would have been more than the troops and landing craft available at the time could have managed. Those with the ultimate responsibility had to be very sure of success: failure would undoubtedly have prolonged the European war into the era, first of the increasingly accurate ballistic missile being developed by the Germans, and then of the nuclear bomb. But the argument is nicely balanced and the shadow of the Second World War and its terrible losses weighed heavily on the Prime Minister and Alan Brooke.

A particular pleasure at the end of 1943 was to see my brother Desmond who arrived in England as a Squadron Leader in the Royal Canadian Air Force. Desmond had suffered from an attack of polio as a small boy and one leg was some two inches shorter than the other, which meant he had to wear a built-up boot. When war seemed likely in 1938, he knew how difficult it would be to get a commission in any of the Services. In consequence, he learned to fly privately and obtained a first-class flying certificate. Armed with this when the time came in 1939, he was able to argue his way into the RCAF as a pilot – a quite exceptional achievement as anyone who has been before a Medical Board will know. He became an outstandingly able pilot, and somewhat unusually also qualified as a navigator. He was used by the RAF at their base at Trenton, Ontario, as an instructor teaching new

1943. 'S' Squadron tanks pass a saluting base.

pilots in what was then the largest training base in the British Empire.

In 1943 he realized his ambition and was posted to the UK to command an operational submarine attack squadron in Coastal Command. This consisted of Wellington Bombers fitted out to attack U-Boats at night, with radar and a searchlight to find them, and depth-charges to sink them. We exchanged visits – he to see our tanks and I to fly with him in his Wellington on a training flight. We got on well, as we had not always done before the War. The five years that we had been apart had allowed us to mature and grow, in a sense, closer.

On my visit to his base in Cornwall, in talking to the pilots in his squadron, they told me they knew when Desmond's plane was coming in to land as he always approached the airfield at high altitude, dived steeply down and flattened out to land. They spoke of him with much affection. The Wellington bomber did well to carry so much specialized equipment, and on taking off was always very well over its permitted payload. These planes played a significant role in the defeat of the U-Boat campaign against our shipping. Night patrols must have been lonely with their endless searching of the inhospitable sea. Desmond and his crew were lost on D-Day, 6 June 1944, reported missing believed killed. We will never know the exact manner of his death, but the boy with polio had grown up to overcome his disability and carry out a role in which he was happy and fulfilled. We owe him, with the others of his crew who gave their lives, a deep debt of gratitude.

To return to the 3rd Battalion Scots Guards. We moved

from Nottinghamshire to Kent prior to the invasion, but my own career had suffered a set-back. When I was promoted to the rank of Major in January 1944 to command one of the three tank squadrons, my pride in my success was to be short-lived. In March 1944, Michael Fitzalan-Howard, who was a few years older and more senior than I, was posted to the battalion from the staff and I reverted to Captain as his Second in Command. The disappointment was a bitter one, made easier by Michael being, and remaining over the years, a good friend.

When the Commanding Officer told me of this decision, he said he was sure it would not be long before I would be called upon again to command a squadron. Sadly – in a sense – he was right, as Sidney Cuthbert, the Battalion Second in Command, was killed on our first day's action in Normandy at the end of July 1944. Willie Whitelaw was promoted to take his place, and I was again to command the Squadron which I knew so well.

In the first few months of 1944, the 6th Brigade was full of rumours that our role was yet again to change, and it was with dismay that shortly before D-Day we lost some of our latest Churchill tanks to another formation, 31st Tank Brigade. Our fate was indeed hanging in the balance to a much greater degree than we could have guessed. When General Montgomery took over command of the Allied Land Forces in preparation for the invasion of Normandy, he considered there was not enough depth of reserves to replace the casualties which the Army would be likely to suffer. He decided that the British forces were not 'well balanced' – in one of his favourite phrases – and that our manpower was too thinly spread over too many units. The army authorities decided in March 1944 that, among other formations, the 6th Guards Tank Brigade should be 'melted down' to provide reinforcement for the Guards Armoured Division.

Had this meltdown happened, it would have been a catastrophe for the officers and men involved. In the case of the 3rd Battalion Scots Guards there was no other tank formation within the Regiment, so the officers and men would have had to be posted as reinforcement drafts to other armoured units in the Guards Armoured, or if the value of their Churchill tank training was to be retained, to Royal Tank Corps units operating Churchill tanks. After three years training together to bring a unit to the highest possible pitch this would have been a tragedy for all those concerned.

Fortunately, there were many supporters willing to take the case of 6th Guards Tank Brigade to the highest level, and indeed in the end the only man who could overrule Montgomery and was prepared to do so, was the Prime Minister. This he did in a reasoned Minute in which he mentioned reinforcements being transferred into the Brigade of Guards from the RAF Regiment, which, incidentally, adopted the ways of the Brigade of Guards well and made good soldiers. Montgomery was furious at being crossed.* Monty wrote to the Director of Staff Duties at the War Office:

---

*Personal Minutes from Churchill to Montgomery of 9.4.44., the miscellaneous correspondence file 21AG/1065/CNC Montgomery Papers held in the Imperial War Museum.

You cannot take line reinforcements and draft them into Guards units just like that. The two disciplines are quite different and it does not work. Meanwhile I have to do something very quickly and the action I have taken is as follows:

(a) I have withdrawn 6th Guards Tank Brigade into Army Group Reserve. This means that it is not in the build-up for Operation OVERLORD [the Normandy landing] and will not be called to France for a long time.

(b) I have replaced it in 2nd Army by 31st Armoured Brigade which was in the Army Group Reserve. One of the regiments is a flame thrower regiment and it suits me very well. I suppose the Prime Minister is within his rights to disregard the considered advice of the Secretary of State for War, Chief of the Imperial General Staff and myself, but I cannot mess up my operations.

[Which is, in fact, exactly what he did.]

He went on to say:

I must have a tidy set-up. I know so well what happens when the set-up is not tidy and is unbalanced. I shall, therefore, not take 6th Guards Tank Brigade to the war.

When Montgomery's biographer, Nigel Hamilton, records this incident, it is a pity he did not also record the outcome of Montgomery's decision. 6th Guards Tank Brigade did not reach Normandy until mid-July 1944. The 15th Scottish Division, with whom they had trained intensively over many, many months, was thus forced to fight in late June in Operation EPSOM with tank formations with whom they had never cooperated, with unhappy results.

When 6th Guards Tank Brigade was used for the first time in the Second Army breakout, Operation BLUECOAT, at Caumont on July 30, it was in cooperation with 15th Scottish Division, and the attack was a formidable success – of which more later.

Montgomery had, in fact, acted out of irritation because his views were being countermanded by the Prime Minister and he had to get his own back. What he did was not in the best interests of the operation. He ignored the years of training which had gone into the Brigade, and between the Brigade and 15th Scottish Division and the difference this would have made in the early Normandy battles. Although Nigel Hamilton does not mention it, Montgomery effectively revised his views of 6th Brigade after their success in the Normandy battle, in particular using them with the 15th Scottish Division for the break-in attacks through the Siegfried Line and the battles up to the Rhine in February 1945. In the following month, he chose the Brigade to be the leading British tank formation to cross the Rhine to join up with the British and American airborne forces and to lead the advance to capture Munster.

The trouble lay to some extent in the faulty projections made by 21st Army Group planners of casualties in the Normandy campaign. Infantry casualties turned out to be much higher, and tank crew and other casualties lower than forecast. In other words, Montgomery had made his decision to melt down the Brigade on a false premise, but, in addition, his reaction of 'taking them out of the build-up' and 'out of the war' was clearly made out of pique and irritation at being overruled.

This set-back in the fortunes of the Brigade had for me a personal implication. Although we battalion officers were never told of our set-back, the long wait from D-Day on 6 June to the middle of July only served to increase our frustration. We do, however, owe to our Commander-in-Chief a certain wry debt of gratitude because had we been involved in the heat of the Normandy battle for those additional five weeks, the number of us who did not return would certainly have been noticeably greater.

The personal outcome was that I received a message to report to Brigade Headquarters in the middle of May 1944 while we were training in Kent prior to the invasion. I was informed by the Brigadier, Gerald Verney, that as the Brigade's arrival in Normandy was to be delayed I had been chosen to go to France attached to XXX Corps Advance Headquarters; I was to take a jeep, a driver and a No. 18 wireless set, and act as a Liaison Officer when required by the Corps Commander, General Bucknall. My personal role, however, was to observe the nature of the tank fighting, talk to those involved, and to report to each of our three battalions before the Brigade embarked for France. Brigadier Gerald Verney did not tell me how long I should stay with XXX Corps Headquarters, nor when the Brigade was scheduled for embarkation – probably because he did not know. I was absolutely delighted at the appointment, and it was with great anticipation that I loaded up a specially water-proofed jeep and set off in May from Battalion Headquarters with my driver, Sergeant Fisher, for briefing at XXX Corps Headquarters in 'The Fort' overlooking Portsmouth.

CHAPTER III

1944 – The D-Day Interlude

It was an exciting drive in the middle of May 1944 from our battalion base near Ashford in Kent – through Southern England, packed almost, it seemed, to bursting point with soldiers, guns, tanks, and every conceivable form of transport – to Portsmouth and 'The Fort' on the high ground overlooking the town which was the headquarters of the 21st Army Group. I eventually found the officer to whom I was to report, John Lewis, at XXX Corps Headquarters – a delightful Major in the Life Guards who made my introduction to this strange world of the Staff very painless. He confirmed that I was to be attached to XXX Corps Headquarters as a Liaison Officer to study the lessons of the early tank fighting in Normandy, and then to return to report to my brigade. I would have the overriding responsibility to act as required by General Bucknall and the staff of XXX Corps Headquarters.

John then took me into the Operations Room where one wall was covered with a vast map of France. There he outlined to me the OVERLORD plan for the invasion of Normandy. When he got to the full role of XXX Corps, he explained that 50th Division was to assault the beaches on

D-Day on Gold Beach on the extreme right of the British/Canadian line, opposite Arromanches, with the objective of reaching Bayeux on D-Day, cutting the main road to Caen and to link with the Canadians on the left and the American US V Corps on the right. Somewhat to my surprise, he told me I was to cross on D-Day (on the second tide) and to help set up the Advance Corps Headquarters. Yet another surprise was that I was to embark on a Canadian LST (Landing Ship Tank) on the east coast at Felixstowe. But, as he outlined the vast scale of the operation, it was clear that more than just the Channel Ports had to be used, although it would mean our convoy from Felixstowe leaving on D-Day Minus One.

I left Portsmouth to report to the heavily isolated camp near Felixstowe the next morning. The secret I was carrying in my head seemed overwhelming. Keeping that secret, and the time and place of the invasion by so many thousands was one of the major security achievements of the War. I know that in my case I was overwhelmed by having the burden of this information suddenly given to me, and having booked into the Guards Club in London for the night, I went out of my way to eat alone in the gloomy dining room and spoke to virtually no-one. In the morning Sergeant Fisher collected me and we set off to Felixstowe to a huge tented camp screened from the outside world, where, some fourteen days before D-Day, we started to load the landing craft.

I was in charge of loading my particular LST, a Canadian one, with the odd assortment of vehicles and tanks which we had to take aboard, the most troublesome of all being three enormous triple-jointed airfield 'scrapers' which were to be used to flatten the ground for forward airfield construction. They seemed to be designed to prevent reversal into confined spaces, and it took all of two days to manoeuvre them snugly into the back of the LST. My own jeep was the last vehicle to load as it was to be the first off – not directly onto the beach, but a few hundred yards away (as it was explained to me) onto a 'rhino ferry', a flat steel platform with two small engines, which was to carry us that short distance to the shore, thus enabling the LST to avoid beaching and return at once to England for the next load.

Apart from loading the LSTs there was very little for me to do, but for the first time in some three years the sense of frustration had disappeared. I was serenely happy to be – at last – on the verge of what we were sure was to be the ultimate battle against Hitler's Germany, the evil nature of which I had no doubt about since my visits to the Nuremberg Party Rally in 1938. I find it difficult to recognize the lack of fighting quality in the British Second Army which Max Hastings describes in his book *Overlord*, nor his assessment of their lack of commitment to battle. He may mistake the well-known preference for understatement of the British against the *'Sieg Heil'* flamboyance of the Germans, whether expressed before, during or after the battle.

One evening there was a concert, or, rather, more of a sing-song, as we had no musicians among us and, of course, no outside entertainers were allowed in. However, we discovered one French Liaison Officer who had a mouth organ, and after the sing-song he ended with a spirited rendering of 'La Marseillaise' and got an enormous ovation.

We were all safely embarked a week before D-Day and I found myself well looked after in the wardroom of the LST by the Canadian naval officers. I was struck by the size and variety of their meals which were on a pre-war scale, and I thought of the severe austerity of civilian rationing in Britain at this late stage of the War, a real hardship of which we in the Forces were much aware, but did not, of course, share.

The days passed slowly – reading, talking and wondering what conditions would be like when we arrived on the second tide on D-Day. Would the plan be fulfilled and the assault of the 50th Division be well inland by the time we landed, or would they be pinned on the beaches? After one recall because of bad weather conditions (Eisenhower's first momentous decision to delay for twenty-four hours), we eventually set off in a large convoy of LSTs on the evening of 5 June and passed through the Straits of Dover at night apparently undetected by German radar, which we now know had been substantially destroyed by Allied bombing. One LST in the convoy was suddenly lit by a huge flash and sank like a stone. Our Captain, with whom I was standing on the bridge at this moment, thought it was 'probably a mine'. There can't have been many survivors for the escorts to pick up.

At dawn we took our place in the armada in the Channel which was indeed awe-inspiring. We went below and busied ourselves checking our vehicles' engines and waterproofing and for once I did not feel seasick despite the rough sea and was able to enjoy our progress across the Channel without any further enemy interference. We had a Catholic chaplain on board and he held Mass on deck for the Catholics among us, and for the first and last time I took part in a silent general confession and a general absolution, followed by Communion. I have the feeling that there were not many atheists or agnostics on board our landing craft.

On the afternoon of D-Day, as we neared the French coast, we were below deck waiting for the ramps to go down but could hear the concentrated noise of unceasing naval bombardment. When the ramps went down, luckily enough there was the rhino ferry on which we had to unload. In the rough sea it was no easy task to judge the moment when to accelerate off the ramp, jump the gap and land on the rhino as it moved up and down in the heaving sea. However, we and the first load of other vehicles following our jeep managed it safely and set off for the beach about 600 yards away. We came to a jarring halt after we had got halfway and found we had run onto one of the German underwater obstacles on which we swung round, firmly pinioned. Luckily, this one had no mine attached to it. The water was too deep to unload our vehicles but some of us swam or waded ashore, although there was nothing we could usefully do until the tide went out.

Gold Beach had been firmly secured, the assault troops having pressed on rapidly inland, and apart from some desultory shelling, the situation seemed unreal – not unlike an exercise, enlivened by strafing by two Messerschmidt fighters, the only enemy air activity we saw. The beach was massively crowded with men and machines being urged forward by the beach masters as they landed from every variety of craft. It was daylight on D-Plus 1 by the time the tide was far enough out for us to manhandle our jeep from the rhino ferry into the water, up to the beach, through the narrow taped exit and onto the road towards Bayeux and to the rendezvous at XXX Corps Advance Headquarters which was in the course of being established with tents and slit trenches in the corner of an orchard.

I felt somewhat of a 'passenger' at Headquarters, although the staff were friendly and helpful. They told me where the armoured units were and who might be able to help in my task of assessing 'lessons in tank fighting'. I was also on occasion used by the Corps Commander as a Liaison Officer.

On 13 June he asked me to go forward and contact the leading Brigade Commander of 7th Armoured Division and find out what was holding up the brigade's advance to Villars Bocage. Sergeant Fisher and I set off up the line of advance, but before long could get no further forward as the lane was jammed nose to tail with tanks and transport bearing the insignia of the Desert Rats of 7th Armoured Division – all stationary. I thanked God for our air superiority, got out of the jeep and walked the length of the nose-to-tail column for a mile or so until I reached the forward Brigade Headquarters. The Brigadier discovered me talking to his Brigade Major, found out that I was General Bucknall's Liaison Officer and, worse still, to his irritation I think, that I was an officer in the Brigade of Guards. He asked furiously for my map and said he would mark it to show the position. Unfortunately, I had left this in the jeep, which made him even more apoplectic. Luckily, I was quickly passed a map by one of his staff on which he outlined what was happening. The leading elements of the Brigade had been badly shot up by Tiger tanks in Villars Bocage, but the Brigade had not been able to react. I realized that no attempt at any outflanking movement had been tried because the Sherman tanks had been unable to get out of or across the sunken lanes; nor, apparently, did they have sufficient infantry to carry out any flanking movement. I returned to Corps Headquarters feeling not a little unlike the Staff Officer in Shakespeare's *Henry IV*, as described so sardonically by Harry Hotspur, when he recommended to Hotspur 'parmaceti for an inward bruise'.

I reported to General Bucknall on my return and told him all I had seen and heard. He was kind enough to say that if all the reports he received were as clear as mine his job would be a lot easier. It was easy to report facts; solutions were more difficult. Montgomery's use of forward Liaison Officers was one of his main means of keeping a grasp on the process of a battle. It might have been wiser if General Bucknall had used this technique more often.

As it was, Montgomery was to replace Bucknall by General Horrocks before the end of the Normandy campaign, as he was also to replace the Commander of 7th Armoured Division, General Erskine, and the Brigadier whose wrath I had incurred – Hinde. General Erskine's replacement was our own 6th Guards Tank Brigadier, Gerald Verney.

The following day I was not needed by XXX Corps, so I went forward in my jeep with Sergeant Fisher in order to make contact with a leading tank squadron I had identified, to try and get more intelligence from them on tactics and the enemy. There was never a front line in Normandy in the First World War sense, but we had quickly learnt the signs to look for whilst moving towards the fighting – the attitude of soldiers, alert or relaxed, and then within the battle area an increasingly deathly quiet, broken only by the sounds of small-arms or shellfire close or far away. Noting the familiar signs, I left the jeep with Sergeant Fisher at the bottom of a small but steep hill on the road leading to Tilly-sur Seulles. Over to the left on the high ground there were Sherman tanks of the squadron I was looking for in what seemed to be a defensive position.

I walked up the lane, avoiding the verge where the German anti-personnel mines were usually laid, to the top of the rise before making off left to see if I could speak to the Tank Commander. As I topped the rise there was the sound of a shell falling very close, and I threw myself into the ditch on the right only to find that at this particular place there was, unusually, no ditch, but only a slight depression of about nine inches. This first shell was closely followed by others, and a full-scale concentration quickly developed of which I was the epicentre. The ground heaved, and the air was full of flying splinters and debris and the all-pervasive smell of cordite. For the first time in the War I was badly frightened, and had to fight back the sensation to get up and run, which would certainly have been the end of me. After a few minutes, or what seemed like a few minutes, the shelling abruptly stopped, and after a pause I gave up the idea of talking to the Tank Commander and walked back down the hill to the jeep.

Right to the end of the campaign I particularly disliked shelling, even in my tank, except in action when there were too many other things to think about. It was an illogical feeling because tank gun and anti-tank gunfire was far more dangerous to a Tank Commander – in fact, even small-arms fire – fighting as he did with his head out of the turret. I have not before mentioned this particular dislike of shelling, and I hope it went unnoticed at the time by others. All tank commanders soon found out that it was not possible to close down the tank turret and follow the course of a tank battle, much less direct it. The only times we closed down under shellfire was when it was heavy and we were stationary and not actively engaged. The tank commanders in our brigade never in fact wore helmets but stuck to the more comfortable beret. (I have noticed that the British UN Commander in Bosnia in 1994/5, General Rose, always wore a beret, never a helmet, nor apparently a flak jacket.)

On reaching the bottom of the hill I found two gunner officers standing by my jeep with Sergeant Fisher who was pleased to see me coming back safe and sound. The two officers welcomed me, and on seeing the Scots Guards flash on my shoulder asked eagerly whether the Guards Armoured Division had landed, and were disappointed with my negative reply. At this second week in the

Normandy campaign, there was a strong feeling on the ground that matters were at a pretty critical point, and any reinforcement, particularly the Guards Armoured Division, would have been very welcome.

Matters were made worse by the very bad weather which delayed the landing of the reinforcements and material. Our old friends, 15th Scottish Division, whom we should have been with, and of whom we had once formed a part, had arrived off the beaches, and General Bucknall wanted to talk to General MacMillan, the Commander, who could not manage to get ashore. He asked me to take a 'DUKW' – a wheeled amphibious vehicle – and fetch him off his transport. Having got hold of a 'DUKW' with some difficulty, I set off from the beach at Arromanches and moved into a moderately rough sea. After scanning a number of ships, I identified the right one, and the tall Major General, in his bonnet, clambered, with difficulty, down a rope ladder into the 'DUKW'. On landing on the beach, the sight of the astonishing profusion of men, equipment and stores had become familiar to me, but it had a different effect on the General. On seeing two privates from the Royal Army Service Corps quietly eating their 'compo' rations at the side of the road, he ordered the driver to stop, leant over and berated these two hapless men many feet below him for not getting on with their job. 'Don't you realize that every moment is vital?' he bellowed, and then drove off watched by two very surprised soldiers.

I did not attend his briefing by General Bucknall, but I was sad at this moment that the 6th Guards Tank Brigade were not landing at the same time as they had been originally scheduled to do, before being pulled out of the order of battle by Montgomery. General MacMillan was a very successful Divisional Commander of the 15th Scottish, a superb division, until he was wounded in August and replaced by General Barber.

Some writers on the Normandy campaign criticize the overdependence on the regimental spirit as part of the reason for, as they describe, the poor fighting quality of the British Army in Normandy. They also cite the Army's lack of dash and poor tactics, arising often from inadequate training and over-reliance on massive tank and artillery support to achieve objectives. My experience bears out little of what they say, qualified by the obvious statement that there were the good and the not so good formations in all the armies engaged. Criticism of the regimental system in my view, as I have said before, is misplaced. Tight-knit units of some 800 officers and men, or at times fewer, were the best size in which to weld a collective pride and induce a high morale. It did not, I believe, as they assert, divide and make cooperation more difficult between units: on the contrary, it in fact made for better cooperation but with a healthy element of competition.

We, as a Churchill tank battalion in the 6th Guards Tank Brigade, were to fight not only with the 15th Scottish Division (with whom we had trained so closely in England), but also with many others – the Infantry Brigade of the Guards Armoured Division, the 3rd Division, the 43rd Division, the 51st Highland Division, the Canadian 3rd Infantry Brigade and the 6th Airborne Division in Normandy, Belgium, Holland and Germany and, finally, across the Rhine with the 17th US Airborne Division. At no time did I feel any disadvantage in the regimental system – very much the reverse: the failings, on the rare occasions when we came across them, were due to the continuing high drain of officer casualties which often left a battalion with just one or two resolute officers, supported by a mixture of the new, inexperienced, and the promoted NCOs who had not always been trained to platoon commander level.

Max Hastings in his book *Overlord* is, however, correct in his criticism of armoured formations training which had been too much based on the lessons of the desert transferred to Salisbury Plain. Endless practising of the 'hull-down' position, which had been the vogue in the desert so that only the turret appeared above the ridge, was totally inappropriate to Normandy 'bocage' tank fighting. On the other hand, the very close tank/infantry coopera-tion which we had worked out with 15th Scottish Division was of immense value in the bocage battle. It reinforces my view, perhaps a partisan one, that Montgomery made a serious error of judgement in his irritation at being overruled by Winston Churchill when he prevented 6th Guards Tank Brigade from going over in June 1944 with 15th Scottish Division. His worries over the erosion of reserves within the British Army were obviously justified, but only in infantry formations: the casualties in tank units, he and the planners had not sufficiently appreciated, would be lighter – much lighter, as I have pointed out – than those in infantry formations. The losses of the tanks themselves could easily be made good.

His proposed meltdown of 6th Guards Tank Brigade to reinforce the Armoured Brigade of the Guards Armoured Division proved, in the event, to have been unnecessary. Both armoured formations ended the campaign in Europe in May 1945 as fully manned and equipped tank fighting units. The story of the infantry with the Guards Armoured Division was a different one. In March 1945, before the Rhine crossing, the 1st Battalion Welsh Guards, the infantry battalion that we supported at Chênedollé in Normandy had suffered such severe casualties that it had to be withdrawn. It was replaced by the 2nd Battalion Scots Guards, brought back from Italy and up to strength by amalgamation with the 4th Battalion Scots Guards – a holding unit – and by reinforcements from the RAF Regiment.

The accounts of 15th Scottish Division in Operation EPSOM at the end of June, and the part played by the supporting Churchill tanks, are well documented. On re-reading these accounts I am more than ever convinced that the employment of 6th Guards Tank Brigade with 15th Scottish Division might have achieved a significantly greater success in this crucial battle in June – Operation EPSOM – to encircle Caen, which came near in any case to achieving a considerable breakthrough across the Orne to the west of the city.

In the account of the British supporting tank operations, related by John Keegan in *Six Armies in Normandy*, the Battalion (our old friends 2nd Argyll and Sutherland Highlanders) had literally to fight their way through Cheux where shut-down tanks were sitting slug-like in the ruins of the main street, while the Battalion's infantry were crossing the start-line, and what little space that was left in the lanes seemed to be filled by our own tanks closed down and deaf to all appeals.

All this fills me with sadness. We should have been there to support our friends. It is not fanciful to believe that a highly-trained and professional 6th Guards Tank Brigade might have succeeded, as they did with 15th Scottish Division in the following month on 30 July, in achieving much greater success. That close bocage country was ideally suited to the superb cross-country performance of the Churchill tanks and enabled them to get within range at which their 75 mm guns were often effective against the better-gunned Panther tank. This factor was seldom exploited in the fighting in June and July, and it is indeed surprising that other Churchill tank brigades were not used in the bocage to greater effect in those early weeks. The battalion which my Squadron had always cooperated with on exercises in the UK was the 2nd Battalion Argyll and Sutherland Highlanders which, totally unsupported by armour, made the crucial advance to capture the bridgehead over the River Odon. Then, having beaten off the German counter-attack and having later been joined by the tanks of 11th Armoured Division, were mistakenly withdrawn behind the river on the Army Commander's order, for reasons we do not know, but probably due to poor communications and to a misreading of the situation.

To return to XXX Corps Headquarters: shortly afterwards I was handed a telegram with the news that my brother Desmond was reported as missing, believed killed, on D-Day. I knew at once that there could be no hope for him, flying as he did on night attack missions against U-Boats far out in the Atlantic. I thought how good a pilot he had been, and how brave to overcome bureaucracy and fly, having, as I wrote earlier, been partially crippled by polio as a boy. I was glad I had been able to see him again and fly with him from his base in Cornwall. His death reinforced the very strong feeling I had had from the beginning of the War that I personally would not survive it. It was not a worry, but a strong premonition – a certainty in my mind. Ever since I have regarded any such premonition, however strong, with considerable scepticism.

After ten days, I became concerned that the Brigade would arrive in Normandy and I would not have done my job of returning to pass on the lessons I had learnt. Nobody at XXX Corps knew when 6th Guards Tank Brigade was scheduled to cross, and eventually I was told by the Corps Commander, General Bucknall, that I should return to England to give them the benefit of my knowledge.

Looking back, I think I made an error in leaving after only two weeks; I should have insisted on staying longer and made greater efforts to discover 6th Guards Tank Brigade's embarkation plan. It did not, in fact, embark at Portsmouth until 16 July, over three weeks later. It would have been better and more informative for everyone if I had been ordered to stay until the Brigade had got its embarkation orders, and then been summoned back.

I was sorry to leave XXX Corps Headquarters, where I had been very well received. I went off with Sergeant

Fisher, leaving our jeep behind, to embark on a returning LSI (Landing Ship Infantry) at the artificially constructed Mulberry Harbour. We had to take a small boat across the harbour. It was a grim place, and as we crossed it three or four swollen bodies floated by and bumped against our boat. They had clearly been killed in the landing and were not in a pleasant state. One body which bumped against the side was turned over by the wash, and with what remained of his face looked up at me – a sight which stayed in my mind for many years. On my return, after stopping briefly in Sussex to tell John Lewis's wife that he was well and in good heart, I arrived back at the Battalion in Kent.

As I walked into the Officers' Mess, Nigel Beeson, the Liaison Captain in 'S' Squadron, who had been standing by the fireplace came forward with mock deference to shake my hand and to say how proud he was at last to be able to shake the hand of an officer of the 3rd Battalion Scots Guards who had been in action. We all laughed, and I started to answer their many questions. Sadly, Nigel Beeson himself was killed the following month in the Battalion's first day's battle in Normandy.

I was anxious to see if I could get forty-eight hours leave to visit the family in Devon whose daughter I had fallen for when I had met her the year before. My Commanding Officer reasonably refused my request because all leave had been banned as embarkation was thought to be only a week away. However, when I went round the Brigade giving my 'talks', I had the opportunity of asking the Brigadier, Gerald Verney, who immediately gave his consent to my request, much, I suspect, to my

Commanding Officer's irritation. We must all have been an insufferable lot in our early to mid-twenties, regarding anyone at the age of thirty-five as probably too old for the job. My two days in Devon were a not uncommon bitter-sweet experience of youth, as my loved one still had half an eye for the dashing MTB officer who had the great advantage of being based close by.

My main interest in life, however, lay with the Battalion, to which I returned to continue to give my views on the lessons of tank fighting. I tried to put across in my talks to the three battalions the necessity to forget at all costs our hull-down training based on manoeuvres on Salisbury Plain and the Yorkshire moors, themselves drawn on Western Desert tactics. In Normandy, the objectives had to be to use the Churchill's cross-country ability (how very great it was I did not fully appreciate at this stage) to get into positions where it could not easily be seen – the corner of a high hedge junction, the side of a barn, house or haystack – with the object of closing the gap between the superior performance of the German 88 mm or long 75 mm guns and our own armament. All this, of course, was an easy and simple doctrine to preach, but often fiendishly difficult to put into practice in battle. We all knew we were decisively out-gunned, but we had, luckily, a superiority in numbers and complete command of the air. We also had great confidence in the reliability and toughness in the cross-country performance of our Churchill tanks – and in our own high professionalism.

When I got back to the Battalion in Kent I found that, among other things, it was in direct line with the stream of

V1 bombs on their way to London, and I learnt to listen for the unmistakable engine note which has been so well compared by John Le Carré to that of a London diesel taxi. A large number of these V1s fell short of London or were shot down en route. One, tragically, scored a direct hit on our brigade's REME workshop killing fifty-one and wounding more than forty. Later in the year, it was a source of great satisfaction when our advance through France, Belgium and Holland overran the sites from which the Germans were launching the V1, and later the V2, rockets.

Walking back across the fields one evening to our headquarters with a colleague in the Battalion, a V1 engine cut out as it passed overhead. My friend threw himself to the ground, but I knew it was going to land a long way ahead and the explosion came from about a mile away. I realized then that even in my short time in Normandy I had started to become what might now be called 'street-wise'.

At long last, on 14 July, the Battalion manoeuvred its tanks onto train flats at Ashford station to take us to Portsmouth for embarkation. As we moved down through Portsmouth to load on the LSTs, and even though the invasion had taken place five weeks before, the people of Portsmouth still crowded the houses on each side of our approach road and waved and cheered us on our way.

CHAPTER IV

Normandy – July and August 1944

When the brigade crossed to Normandy in mid-July, the military situation was nearing the point of decision. Operation GOODWOOD was about to be launched to the east of Caen, and although it failed to achieve a breakthrough it tied down the bulk of the German Panzer divisions. The failure to break out resulted in severe criticism at the highest Anglo-American level, partly due to Montgomery's over-optimism before and during the battle. This led to a plot, orchestrated mainly by Tedder, to get Montgomery sacked. Fortunately, Alan Brooke, the CIGS, was there to give his constant support and occasional guidance to his immensely able, but often tactless Commander-in-Chief. This, and the development of the military situation as Monty had forecast, saved his position and largely his reputation.

The start of the American breakout operation on the right, Operation COBRA, followed on 25 July, and after two weeks of bitter fighting in the bocage the way was being made for the breakout and, eventually, the headlong advance by General Patton. Montgomery saw it was vital in mid-July that the effort of the Second Army be quickly swung away

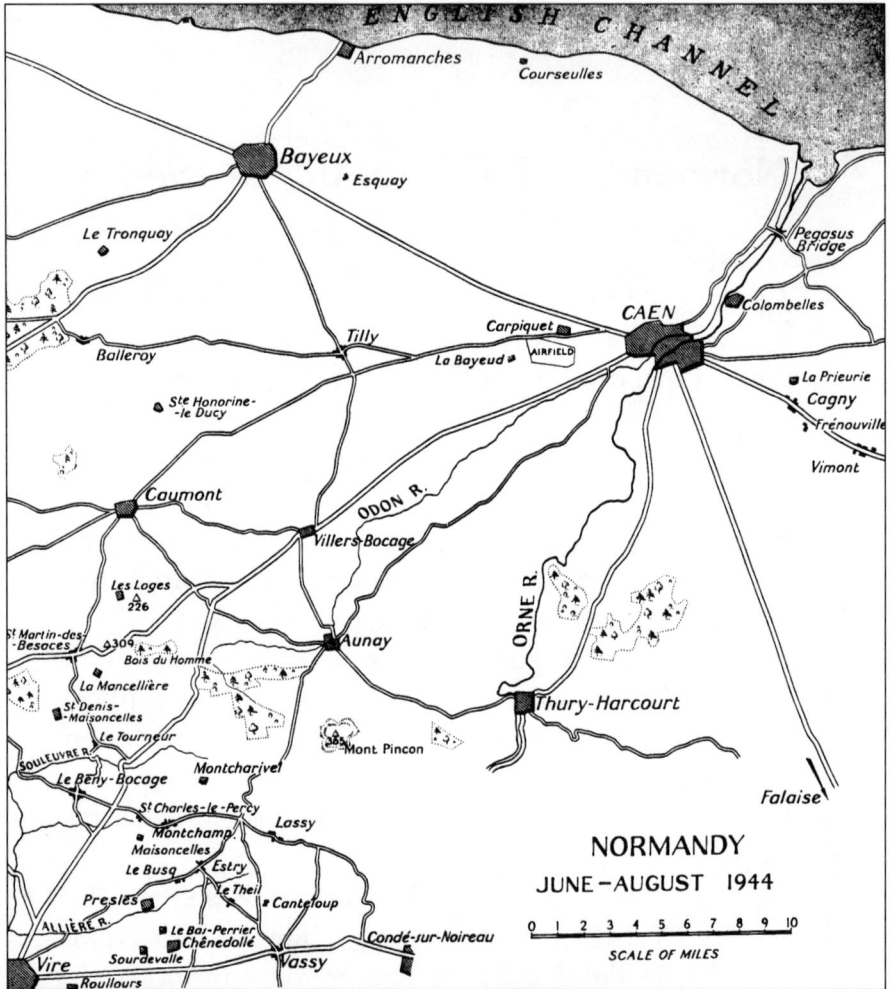

Map showing the Normandy region, labelled with locations including Arromanches, Courseulles, Bayeux, Esquay, Le Tronquay, Balleroy, Tilly, Carpiquet, La Bayeud, Airfield, Ste Honorine-le Ducy, Pegasus Bridge, CAEN, Colombelles, La Prieurie, Cagny, Frénouville, Vimont, Caumont, Villers-Bocage, ODON R., Les Loges 226, St Martin-des-Besaces, Bois du Homme, La Mancellière, Aunay, ORNE R., St Denis-Maisoncelles, Le Tourneur, Mont Pincon, Thury-Harcourt, Montcharivel, Le Beny-Bocage, St Charles-le-Percy, Montchamp, Lassy, Maisoncelles, Le Busq, Estry, Presles, Le Theil, Canteloup, ALLIERE R., Le Bas-Perrier, Chênedollé, Sourdevalle, Vassy, Condé-sur-Noireau, Vire, Roullours, SOULEUVRE R., Falaise

ENGLISH CHANNEL

NORMANDY

JUNE – AUGUST 1944

0 1 2 3 4 5 6 7 8 9 10

SCALE OF MILES

Advance from Caumont to Vire-Vassy road.

from the east of Caen onto the extreme right at the junction of the British and American forces and the hinge of the German line and, importantly, the division between the two German armies in the west. This hinge had to be broken if the dangers of a German counter-attack against the flank of the American advance were to be met. The British attack was commanded by General Dempsey, Commander of the 2nd Army, using XII and XXX Corps, and, for the first time in hard bocage fighting, significant and rapid advances were made. The role of 6th Guards Tank Brigade in this, their first operation, was crucial and was to support their old friends, 15th Scottish Division, in their attack south from Caumont. The 3rd Battalion Scots Guards were to support 227 Brigade, and 'S' Squadron, 2nd Battalion Argyll and Sutherland Highlanders. A long night approach march preceded the attack on 30 July.

I had returned to my role as Second in Command of Left Flank Squadron, and was sad over my lost command as we clattered our way slowly along the Normandy lanes, but pleased to be back with the Battalion for its first battle. It was difficult to stay awake on those long night approach marches. The driver was busy keeping a steady distance from the tank in front, the tank gunner and wireless operator were asleep in the turret; and the Tank Commander, standing with his head out of the turret or slightly lower – almost asleep – waking when his head fell forward with a bang against his periscope, and then perhaps to help them both stay alert, having a word with the driver on the intercom.

As the Battalion deployed and moved up to the start line,

Lancaster bombers streamed overhead dropping, we were told, some 1,000 tons of bombs onto the final objective, the far ridge some 5 miles ahead, covering it in clouds of smoke and dust. It was an encouraging sight, but it is very doubtful if it had any effect on the immediate outcome of the battle although by a lucky chance the German Divisional Commander's HQ was hit.

Left Flank Squadron was in reserve moving up behind the two leading squadrons who were with the Scottish infantry. We had struck an area held by the German 326th Division, a formation of medium quality supported by the 2nd Panzer Division. The Scottish infantry were slowed up by the close nature of the country and machine-gun pockets of determined resistance. The tanks were ordered not to wait for the infantry mopping up, but to go forward to their objective, the ridge at Les Loges some 4–5 kilometres into enemy territory. This ridge was one of the few fairly open features in the middle of the thick bocage country and not likely to be a very healthy spot in light of the inevitable German counter-attack. However, it was the decreed objective and the Battalion reached it with 'S' Squadron on the left and Right Flank on the right. Left Flank Squadron was echeloned behind them on a heavily wooded ridge half a mile or so to their rear – all with no infantry support at this stage.

It was on this first advance that we discovered the Churchill tank's extraordinary ability to cross the highest banks, ditches, and lanes of the bocage – shatteringly uncomfortable although it was to the crew as each climb was followed by a crashing pitch forward.

This was the only day in the campaign in which I was to fill the role of the Squadron Second in Command, and I was glad that it was the only one. There were four squadron headquarters tanks. The Squadron HQ troop usually moved in a diamond formation with the Squadron Commander at the point, the Second in Command and the Liaison Captain to his right and left, and the Squadron Sergeant-Major echeloned behind the Squadron Commander.

The Second in Command and the Squadron Sergeant-Major had the dubious distinction of their tanks being armed with a 3" howitzer which was only ever used, in our experience, to fire smoke shells. The Second in Command was very much the 'spare wheel', with no immediate responsibilities. I had at least time to observe at leisure what was developing in front of us, which was indeed a very unpleasant situation.

One by one I saw the forward tanks of 'S' Squadron enveloped in flames or smoke as they burnt in turn. We could not see where the fire was coming from and no information came back on the battalion wireless net. We normally worked on a battalion net and consequently each tank in the Battalion knew what was going on. With good wireless discipline the net did not get overloaded and control worked well. There was a subsidiary 'B' set for close communication.

As one tank after another burst into flames, or in one or two cases actually blew up, we heard the voice of the Commanding Officer over the air saying to Sidney Cuthbert, the Battalion Second in Command, 'Go over and see what is happening on the left.' As Sidney moved across in his tank he was hit and the tank exploded into a mass of flame blowing the turret some way from the hull. My glasses at this moment (the height of the attack) were trained on Nigel Beeson's tank, and I saw him draw himself out of the turret of his burning tank only to be hit by a bullet or shell splinter and fall beside the tank. Twelve of 'S' Squadron's sixteen tanks were destroyed, Sidney Cuthbert's making the thirteenth.

As we watched, out from the smoke and over the ridge came two very large German tanks, the Commander of the leading one standing well out of his turret waving his arms, whether as a signal or as a gesture of triumph I could not tell. They veered to our left and out of sight into the woods bordering the Les Loges ridge. They were shot at by our Squadron, and the Liaison Captain, Captain Peter Balfour, may have scored a hit on one. The Gunner Forward Observation Officer with 'S' Squadron, whose tank had been knocked out, said that he saw the German Tank Commander (who passed close by him as he lay on the ground) standing well out of his turret and laughing, presumably at the ease of the destruction he had caused.

We now know these two to have been JAGD Panthers. It was a cruel stroke of ill luck for the Battalion, and for 'S' Squadron in particular, that two or possibly three such formidable tank destroyers were positioned in the wood on the flank of the advance covering the objectives at Les Loges. The JAGD Panther was a self-propelled gun, a tank destroyer with the very latest model of 88 mm gun, the KWK 43/3L/71, and heavy front and side armour. The only other German tank to mount this latest 88mm was the King Tiger, the Panzer VIB. The JAGD Panther had only gone into production at the beginning of 1944, and was not even on the tank identification chart issued before the invasion. We now know that they were part of a unit of twelve JAGD Panthers of the 654th GHQ Anti-Tank Battalion, the only such unit in the German Army in the West. Why these two or three latest and heaviest tank destroyers were deployed at this point in the German order of battle, in what had been up to our attack that morning a quiet sector, I have been unable to discover.

However we were in one sense fortunate in that these tank destroyers having just come into service had only had a very brief period of training near Paris. Had they been more highly trained and better commanded they would have held their position at the edge of the wood, or moved a hundred yards or so to their left and engaged Right Flank Squadron with what might well have been similar devastating results.

As they disappeared, they left the open ground covered in burning tanks. There was nothing I could personally do at this stage, so I asked the Squadron Commander, Michael Fitzalan-Howard, if I could take my hull gunner and go on foot to see if we could discover where the two JAGD Panthers had gone. He agreed. We armed ourselves with a Sten gun each and grenades from our tank and set off on foot. As we got to the bottom of the slope we met some of the survivors of the burnt-out tanks from 'S' Squadron making their way back, many of them wounded. 'S' Squadron Second in Command, Billy Bull – who was one of them as his tank had been knocked out – told me later that they were encouraged by the sight of us going off on our little stalking mission, as it had seemed to them that their whole world had fallen in. We followed a track through the woods for half a mile or so, but finding nothing – not even tank tracks – returned to the Squadron. We should perhaps have gone further as were told that the two JAGD Panthers were found many days later abandoned deep in the woods. They had probably run out of petrol. On the whole it was probably not a very wise foray, as our left flank was completely open as 7th Armoured Division had failed to make progress.

On my return to the Squadron, I had a message to report to the Commanding Officer. He told me of Sidney Cuthbert's death and that Willie Whitelaw was to be Battalion Second in Command, so I was promoted to Major again to take command of 'S' Squadron. He reminded me that earlier in the year he had told me it would not be long before I was once again in command of a squadron. I replied truthfully that Sidney's death was far too high a price to pay. Sidney had been a good friend, and had enormously improved and enlivened our years of training. He was a man of great enthusiasm and a propounder of wonderfully experimental ideas. When it was pointed out to him that his schemes were perhaps impractical, he would throw back his head and laugh delightfully – a laugh which, over fifty years later, I would instantly recognize. The sadness of his death was compounded by the fact that, when his tank had exploded, he and his crew had been completely incinerated so that not even their identity discs could be found. He therefore had to be reported as missing, believed killed. This was the only time that our Churchill tanks exploded in this way on being hit by anti-tank fire. Whether it was due to the relatively short range or the high velocity of the latest model of 88 mm gun in the JAGD Panther, we do not know.

The success of the attack at Caumont, not only by 3rd Scots Guards and the Argyll and Sutherland Highlanders, but also by the rest of 15th Scottish Division and 6th Guards Tank Brigade, and eventually by 11th Armoured Division on our right, resulted in a deep break into the German position. It forced the German High Command to react in the next few days by deploying 9th and 10th SS Panzer Divisions who had lately been switched from the Russian front and were now in the Caen sector. This was a significant help to the American advance down the Cherbourg Peninsula, which was beginning to achieve the long-awaited breakout, but whose left flank was vulnerable. The additions of 9th and 10th SS Panzer Divisions to the German counter-attack at Mortain could have proved crucial. General Dempsey described the Caumont breakthrough by the British Second Army as being one of the decisive battles of the European campaign.

The official report on the actions of the British Second Army in Normandy is one of the most prosaic and understated documents that I have read, but even it says: 'There can be no doubt that a large measure of the success achieved in the opening phase is attributable to the magnificent cooperation between the 15th Scottish Division and the 6th Guards Tank Brigade.'

Back in the Squadron we had been taken out of battle to refit, and the next six days were devoted to reconstructing the Squadron in tanks and men. I was lucky enough to have officer replacements available. Of the two captains, Billy Bull had survived and Charles Graham was shortly to arrive to replace Nigel Beeson who had been killed. Of the four troop commanders, Tony Stevenson and Peter Hickling survived; Peter Ward arrived to replace Dick Humble who had been killed, and Cyril Cunningham, who had been very badly wounded, was replaced by Michael Law. Fortunately, Squadron-Sergeant Major Todd, although his tank had been knocked out, was unhurt and, as always, his support was invaluable. There were not a few battalion cooks, mess orderlies and 15 cwt truck drivers who suddenly found themselves co-opted as tank crew to make up the forty casualties, half of our tank crew strength.

On 8 August after one week I was able to bring the new squadron back into the Battalion, the other two squadrons having fought one more battle in our absence at Estry, against a battle group of the newly-arrived 10th SS Panzer Division, which had been indecisive, but in which Graham Mathieson, Liaison Captain in Alan Cathcart's Right Flank Squadron had been killed. Estry showed the determination and fighting skill of the SS Divisions who, despite heavy losses, had established extremely effective battle groups with that quick reaction to changing circumstances at which the German Army was adept.

On the return of the Squadron to the Battalion we celebrated with a hilarious party, and I was glad to see that morale was high. Regimental Headquarters was written to:

'"S" Squadron rejoined us today with an absolutely first-class team – Charles Farrell, Billy Bull and Charles Graham.'

Now for the first and last time in the campaign in North-West Europe, 6th Guards Tank Brigade and the Guards Armoured Division, of which they had originally formed part, cooperated together in the final stage in this sector of the breakout battle in Normandy. The considerable advance south by the Second Army from Caumont successfully put great pressure on the German Army which was attempting to mass in order to attack and cut off the American advance down the Cherbourg Peninsula into Brittany. In order to protect themselves from the Second Army thrust, the Germans, as we have seen, had among others moved 9th and 10th SS Panzer Divisions and one Tiger tank battalion to cut off this advance through the bocage. It was a battle group from these troops which was in position at our next objective at Le Haut Perrier and Chênedollé on the vital Perrier ridge dominating the Vire-Falaise Road. At Chênedollé and Le Haut Perrier the squadron role was to support two companies of 1st Battalion Welsh Guards in their attack on Le Bas Perrier, then to support the infantry battalion of the Coldstream Guards to a further exploitation to dominate the line of the Vire-Vassy-Falaise road.

The battle was to be the test of the newly reformed squadron. I was much aware of this as Peter Leuchars, the Subaltern commanding (due to casualties) the Welsh Guards Company, and I set out in my jeep to make the initial reconnaissance. From my experience in putting together the new squadron, I was conscious of the thinness of our immediate reserves of officers and men, but above all knew that we had to fight hard and successfully in order to show what we could achieve, and last but not least to try to avenge the heavy losses at Caumont.

It was a hot afternoon that 10th of August as our jeep crawled up the Normandy lane towards the ridge ahead, past Le Bas Perrier and the 'Dust Bring Shells' signs. There was an absolute stillness, often a warning of passing forward positions and drawing close to the enemy. Peter Leuchars and I left the jeep at the bottom of the steepish incline and walked warily and slowly up the lane alongside the hedge to get a closer look at the orchard where we were to form up for the attack at dawn the following day. We knew that the enemy holding the crest of the ridge at Le Haut Perrier in front of us were part of 10th SS Panzer Division, but we had not been told that any action had taken place before over this ground, nor that Chênedollé was their central strong point on the Perrier ridge. To our surprise, as we looked over the hedge to our right, we saw that our attack would not indeed be the first. There were two lines of grotesquely swollen bodies in British battledress lying face down at a few yards intervals wearing the shoulder flashes of the Warwickshire Regiment. They had obviously been caught by machine-gun fire advancing in open order.

The place had an evil air, the stench of death was strong and it was deadly quiet. The ridge had in fact been fought over by 11th Armoured Division and elements of the 3rd Division, and lost to 10th SS Panzer Division four days before. In 1994 on a battlefield tour with the Welsh Guards on the 50th Anniversary of the landings, I met the Mayor of the little village of Le Haut Perrier at a celebration dinner. He was ten years of age in August 1944 and his father was the Mayor. While sheltering in the cellar they had heard the sound of fighting above and around them, and then there was the sound of tanks coming up the lane to their farm.

Imagining liberation they ran out to wave a welcome, only to discover the tanks were German SS Panzers, and they fled back into their cellar where they remained unharmed over the next few days' fighting – fighting which completely destroyed their home and farm buildings. When I said at our dinner that I was sorry for the destruction we had caused to his home, he said, 'On the contrary: it is for us to thank you for fighting for us and for our freedom.'

Having discovered the best forming-up area for the attack in the orchard on the left of the road, we returned to our respective order groups – Peter Leuchars to No. 3 Company, 1st Battalion Welsh Guards, and I to my own Squadron. Planning went on for most of the night: the order groups with the Welsh Guards and then with my own Squadron, the left half of the Squadron being commanded on this occasion by my Second in Command, Billy Bull, supporting No. 2 Company of the Welsh Guards. There was time for just one hour's sleep. Reveille was 1.30 a.m. and we had to move out on the approach march at 3.30 a.m. in order to get on the start line at 5.30 a.m. in good time for our scheduled attack at H-Hour, 6.30 a.m.

The Welsh Guards had taken up their positions on the night before, 10 August, and relieved the 2nd Battalion Warwickshire Regiment. The slit trenches, which had to be deepened by the taller guardsmen, were on a slope in an orchard in deep bocage country looking up towards the German-held ridge at Le Haut Perrier. The Warwickshires were pleased to be relieved and wasted no time in getting out. They had been detached to support 11th Armoured Division in their breakout toward Vire, and had met, head on, 9th and 10th SS Panzer Divisions moving to block the yawning gap in the German line of defence. They suffered severely in the fighting, and in the six days before their relief by the Welsh Guards, had casualties of no less than seven officers and 195 men. In the next three days' fighting against elements of the German 3rd Paratroop Division, from 13 August, they were to lose another three officers and eighteen men, including the last surviving Company Commander who had landed with them on D-Day. These figures illustrate the incessant drain of casualties on an infantry battalion in the Normandy fighting.

The Welsh Guards company, under the command of Lieutenant Peter Leuchars (to become a Major General after the War), has suffered severely since landing in Normandy. The company Second in Command was Lieutenant John Reid in his first battle, sadly to be killed by mortar fire in the first few minutes of the attack. David Stevenson, a young Second Lieutenant who had only joined the Battalion a few days before, commanded one platoon and the other two were commanded by sergeants.

Peter Leuchars said much later that his commanders

had been concerned that 'they were fielding what might be described as a third eleven'. They certainly did not fight like a third eleven; they were brave, dogged and resourceful.

On my return to the Squadron I crawled under my tank to lie down to snatch an hour's sleep. I was always by far the last of the crew to crawl underneath due to pressure of order groups. It was always to find that Sergeant McInder, my tank gunner, and Sergeant Adair, my wireless operator, had brought from the the tank my small pack and laid out my sleeping bag. One could not have had better friends or a more able turret crew. Sleep within the battle area, besides being at a premium, was always in a pit which was dug and the tank driven over it to provide what was a snug and usually shell-proof sleeping area. Some have said that this method was considered dangerous as the tank could sink on soft ground and crush the crew. We had no instance of this happening, but on one occasion an officer and his crew were killed by a shell which landed unluckily in the few inches gap between the front of their tank and into the dugout pit.

We left the concentration area as planned at 3.30 a.m., and after an approach march on which one tank broke down, were ready to cross the start line in the orchard at 5.30 a.m. As the second hand on my watch came up to 6.30 a.m. I gave the order for the tanks to advance. As I did so, very heavy German 'mortaring' began causing casualties to the Welsh Guards infantry.

The Welsh Guards had never trained in close infantry/tank cooperation which was our normal mode of fighting, but the plan we worked out with them was to prove successful. They told us later that one of the things which took them by surprise was the appalling noise of fighting so closely with tanks – the din of the tracks and the engines, and the constant firing of 75 mm guns and BESA machine-guns from each tank. We were very confident of our skills and training, and my main concern, knowing we were up against an SS Panzer battle group, was to pinpoint the position of the enemy armour and destroy them.

In the first minutes of moving forward, it was clear from the ferocity of the shelling and the intensity of the fire from the German MG 42s, which had started up immediately, that we were in for a tough time from this battle group of the 10th SS Panzer Division. The Welsh Guards company were pinned down and suffered casualties from continuing accurate mortar fire to their already depleted numbers. Shortly afterwards, Michael Law's tank, which was about twenty yards in front of mine, was knocked out by a source he sadly did not identify, and it was not until after the battle that we discovered that a 75 mm round from one of the Panther tanks had penetrated his forward sprocket wheel and track, and not, as we had first thought, a mine which had disabled his tank. He was forced to evacuate, using the escape hatch on the side closest to my tank, and his five-man crew took cover.

The Welsh Guards then decided to switch their attack round to the left in the hope that progress might be easier there. One of their officers spoke to me on the intercom on the back of my tank to ask if I could swing it round to block a gap in the high bank, thus allowing the Welsh Guardsmen a shelter behind which to cross and switch the direction of their attack. This I did, and gave them the protection from the machine-gun fire to cross the gap. One small party consisting of an officer, a Sergeant and two men fought their way forward into the farmhouse building, but the German tanks firing from point blank range killed the Sergeant through the wall of the house and the others were forced to fall back.

The vital information breakthrough came when Peter Hickling, the Troop Commander on the left, by stretching well out of his turret above the line of the hedge, spotted three Panther tanks in the farmyard at Le Haut Perrier some 150 yards away. It was a good effort to have seen without being seen, and at last we knew where the important opposition was. There was incidentally no question of our Tank Commanders closing the turret hatch down as they would have had to use only their periscope and would have lost control. Although I was being careful to give the Germans a minimal target, the incessant noise from the inside of the tank – that is to say, the noise of the MG 42 bullets striking the turret – was, of course, loud for my gunner and wireless operator. At this moment there was a pull at my sleeve and a short comment from Sergeant Adair, my wireless operator: 'Don't be so f. . .ing bolo,* Sir', which of course I was not being. For the wireless operator and gunner inside the tank there was little means of knowing what was happening except for the sound of our

---

*'bolo', battalion slang for foolhardy.

own guns and the bullets of the enemy machine-guns striking us – the tank periscopes gave a very inadequate vista. Also my crew did not know that because of the steep angle of the ground I could keep the front of the turret between me and the MG42 fire.

Unknown to me at the time, but reported by the Welsh Guards after the battle, our one broken-down tank then joined us in the middle of the battle and, not having made contact, drove straight up the sunken lane into the enemy position at Le Haut Perrier to be knocked out by the waiting Panthers. A Welsh Guards sergeant saw the tank go past him, thought the battle was won, but then heard the explosion as the tank was hit. Shortly afterwards, the Sergeant Tank Commander returned down the lane, borrowed a PIAT (the hand-held anti-tank weapon) from the Welsh Guards and went back to try to destroy the Panther, but sadly came back wounded with a broken PIAT. One other crew member, the driver, with his legs shattered, dragged himself down the lane and was taken by the Welsh Guards to their regimental aid post where he died. This close fighting between Le Bas and Le Haut Perrier lasted some four hours.

An Extract from Welsh Guards at War by Major C.F. Ellis (1946) describes the incident:

> While the smoke lasted the company could see little, but the Scots Guards tanks worked out to their left, spotted three Panthers moving and promptly knocked out all three. No 3 Company was loud in praise of the work done by the 3rd Battalion Scots Guards that day. Even when the tanks were hit (they lost two) they came and joined the infantry.

One Lance Sergeant borrowed No 7 Platoon's Piat to go and deal with a Panther which had knocked out his tank. He came back with his hand bleeding and the Piat in pieces. He then grabbed a rifle and went back again. That was the last of him. Another driver with both legs blown off was incredibly brave.

After the village was occupied the Welsh Guards History goes on:

Among the broken, battered and burning houses in the village and tattered remnants of apple trees which had been green and peaceful a few hours before, lay two Panthers well alight, and a third with a neat hole through its turret with the engine still running and its wireless working. They were part of the Scots Guards bag.

Once we had been able to identify the position of the German tanks I had ordered Peter Ward's troop across from the left where the attack had gone forward more easily. He moved cautiously, and by a splendid effort on his part was able to get within 150 yards and knock out all three of the Panther tanks as the *Welsh Guards History* describes. On this success the balance of the engagement swung decisively in our favour. Opposition at Le Bas Perrier lessened, the SS infantry started to pull back and, after consulting Peter Leuchars, I swung the full Squadron round further to the left and advanced, by-passing Le Haut Perrier, on towards our final objective with the Coldstream Guards past Chênedollé overlooking the important road between Vire and Vassy. Looking back, it would have been more effective if I had earlier swung the whole of the left of the Squadron across to cut off the remains of the withdrawing SS battle group weakened by the loss of their tanks. The basic trouble was that we were not a properly integrated battle group, but were under the command of the Welsh Guards infantry companies who did not have the communications to control the battle. This is not a criticism of their efforts in battle, which were beyond all praise; the fact was that we had never worked together before and they had not been trained in close infantry/tank cooperation. Our success was all the sweeter for that.

The Coldstream Guards infantry company was delayed and had not appeared on the start line, and therefore we advanced across rough bocage country as a full squadron without tank or gun opposition, to our final objective. There was intermittent machine-gun fire, and one of our tank commanders, Sergeant Macfarlane, was killed by a bullet through the head. I gave the crew permission to pass his body out of the side escape hatch as they could not fight the tank with his body in it. We eventually made contact with the Coldstream Battalion on our objective, and sat dominating the Vire-Vassy road a few hundred yards in front of us.

On our right John Mann, commanding the Squadron in the absence of Alan Cathcart who had been injured in a fall, was supporting the 5th Battalion Coldstream Guards. He told me afterwards how impressed he had been by the steadfastness and determination of the Coldstream company commanded by Billie Hartington, who he had been at school with. He described Billie walking bare-headed on that hot August afternoon swinging his steel helmet in his hand and unconcernedly directing his Company forward. He was to be killed the following month commanding his Company in the attack on Heppen at the beginning of the drive for Nijmegen and Arnhem.

That had been a good day for the Squadron. We had come back from shattering losses at Caumont and helped significantly to defeat an SS Panzer battle group with the loss of two tank commanders and two tanks knocked out, and had helped win the vital ridge dominating the Vire-Falaise road. We learnt later that when the Welsh Guards advanced to the far side of Haut Perrier and Chênedollé they mopped up the remaining SS troops, captured nine and killed others. They had one more surprise that day. An hour later a Panther tank, probably cut off from its retreat by our advance, came lumbering back up the lane into the Welsh Guards' position. They only had one PIAT left to deal with it thanks to our Sergeant's earlier effort. The first two rounds missed, the third (their last) hit the tank and, to their surprise (there was little confidence in the PIAT) it started to catch fire and the crew started to bail out, three were killed as they emerged and one escaped into the bocage.

In 'S' Squadron, after some fourteen hours in our tanks, we were relieved to be ordered to return to the forward rally area. We were well received by the Commanding Officer; in fact, he was jumping up and down with excitement over this, a proven success for the Battalion against enemy tanks. There was some shelling in the evening, and the Squadron suffered one or two casualties of which I knew little because, after reporting to the Commanding Officer and seeing to the refuelling and re-ammunitioning, I had, utterly exhausted, lain down beside my tank and fallen asleep. It was not until later that I heard from Squadron Sergeant-Major Todd that one of our tank commanders, a Lance Sergeant, was found by him crouching at the bottom of the turret of his tank on his return to the 'laager' having lost his nerve. Sergeant-Major Todd had, with difficulty, got him out and into the medical half-track for evacuation. No action was taken against him. We had learnt a lot and changed our methods of dealing with mental 'breakdown' since the First World War.

The battle had been a success, and the newly constituted Squadron had 'sweet revenge', as the Scots Guards history says, on that day around Le Haut Perrier and Chênedollé. I was happy with the result as our casualties were light – two killed and three wounded – and only two tanks lost. We and the Welsh Guards Company, who of course suffered very much heavier casualties, together defeated a strong battle group from 10th SS Panzer Division.

The Panther tank, which the Welsh Guards found with a small hole in the forward part of its turret, was in perfect working and fighting order – the SS withdrawal had abandoned it somewhat prematurely.

We repainted the tank with allied identification and took it with us when we moved forward to cross the Seine. Sadly, the radiator was allowed to run dry and the engine seized up – I would have liked to have had it with us in our later battles as its long 75 mm was a better gun than anything we had.

It was a pity that the breakthrough achieved by the Second Army against this hinge of the German defence in Normandy was not exploited as it might have been. This may have been because the command structure, which had worked well under Montgomery, was about to revert to Eisenhower, and Montgomery's control of the land battle was beginning to loosen.

Our forces, which had broken through in this area around Vire, could have been employed in swinging round to reinforce the short hook and help the encirclement of the German armies in the Falaise Gap. Despite desperate fighting by the Canadian Army and the Polish Armoured Division towards Falaise, and the enormous damage done by the Allied air attacks in the Falaise Gap, substantial German forces, both armoured and infantry, succeeded in crossing the Seine and eventually rejoining the battle. It has been estimated by John Keegan that no fewer than 25,000 vehicles and 300,000 men were successfully ferried by the German forces across the Seine to escape to the north. Nevertheless the scale of the victory over the German Army in Normandy ranks with any other, including Tunisia and Stalingrad. However, had the noose been closed, it is doubtful whether the German Army in the West could have survived as it did for another nine months of campaigning until May 1945. It was the remnants of the 9th and 10th SS Panzer Divisions who were unfortunately refitting at Arnhem the following month.

In this battle, as in others we fought in, before and later, I saw no reflection in the infantry we cooperated with of the 'flawed instrument' theory so widely written of by many writers in their description of the British forces in the campaign which they contrast with the performance of the German troops. There were, in my view, in fact, on both sides in Normandy the very good, the good and the mediocre. The Germans, in their SS Divisions and some Panzer Divisions, had a high proportion of very good troops. Quality is, after all, based on first-rate discipline, a high standard of training and first-class weapons, which will be reflected in a high morale and performance.

The British soldier in Normandy laboured under serious disadvantages: in the infantry his training had not focussed on the thick bocage country in which he found himself, his Bren was seriously inferior in rate of fire to the MG 42, his personal anti-tank weapon, the PIAT, was markedly inferior to the German Panzerfaust, as was his personal automatic weapon, the Sten, as against the German Schmeisser. Most importantly, there were far too few of him. Although our manpower was stretched to the limit, the Army maintained to the end a massive administrative 'tail', not as large as the American but very much greater than the German. As I have said it took over twice as many men to put one man into battle as it should have done, using the German ratio.

In armour, whether in the Armoured Division or in the Tank Brigade, our tanks were markedly inferior – out-gunned and out-armoured. It usually took a squadron of British or American tanks to deal with three or four Tigers or Panthers. In anti-tank weapons, although the British 17-pounder was an excellent gun, it was in far too few tanks; and SP guns – the German 88 mm – was all too often the arbiter of the tank battle, whether in a self-propelled chassis such as the JAGD Panther, in a tank, the Tiger, or when operating as a static field piece. Only in the artillery did we have the advantage, but this was to some extent counter-balanced by the superior rate of fire and accuracy of their mortars.

Fortunately, these manifest disadvantages were taken in their stride by most of those involved in the fighting. Those who had spent years training in England were eager to prove themselves as first-class professional soldiers. I do not recognize the picture of the reluctant participant in the invasion which some writers paint. Divisions which had fought through North Africa and Italy, such as 51st Highland Division and 7th Armoured, were suffering from a degree of war weariness, but so were many of the German divisions.

A typical example of our wretched war planning in the weapon field was our failure to develop our excellent 3.7-inch anti-aircraft gun in an anti-tank role. Thousands of these guns were available during 1944 and 1945 and, thanks to our total air superiority, they were virtually unused. They should have been developed as ground anti-tank guns and mounted on a tracked chassis – particularly with the clear example of the German success with their 88 mm, in front of our eyes since 1942. The other astonishing factor is this failure to redeploy Anti-Aircraft Command, which was employing in July 1944 in manpower the equivalent of ten infantry divisions.

These are questions which military historians might examine, and they might give clearer answers as to why the

German Army was able to perform against us in battle as well as it did in 1944 and 1945. Perhaps the British talent for understatement (of the officers interviewed, less notable in some of our generals) may have misled later writers into underrating the dogged determination of the British infantry soldier and what he achieved in Normandy.

Our total air superiority, of course, did much to counteract the German ground weapon superiority. Its main effect was, however, felt in its massive destructive power against the German line of communications, in preventing them from moving their troops by day at will from one sector to another. Its close support role was on the whole sadly lacking, mainly because the leading figures in the RAF did not believe in it and thought it a digression from their main task of bombing Germany into submission. Thus, when close support was given, it was often unpracticed and very apt to be at the expense of our own troops. When very clear and large targets presented themselves, as they did in the Falaise Gap, then our total control of the air of course paid very great dividends.

On a personal note, my tank squadron was only attacked from the air three times, in the course of the campaign, always by our own side – twice by low-level bombing (USAF and RAF) and once by RAF rocket-firing Typhoon fighters. The latter were particularly concentrated in their efforts – but all missed their targets.

After the conclusion of the Normandy fighting the Battalion had a short break while we refitted and waited for orders to move forward again. Some of us took advantage of this opportunity to travel around, and the three squadron commanders, Alan Cathcart, John Mann (having succeeded Michael Fitzalan-Howard who had moved to a Staff appointment) and I, went first to Rennes where we were unable to get a meal, but had a rousing reception as we were the first British troops the townspeople had seen. Our trip, a day or two later, to Paris was not entirely successful, as although Rupert D'Oyly Carte, Chairman of the Savoy Hotel Group in London, had given Alan 'introductions' to the Hotel Meurice, our expectations of a good meal were disappointed. The Manager took us down to the kitchens and showed us their completely empty larders – undoubtedly a reaction of their neighbours to the hotel having been requisitioned and used as the German military headquarters! However, the Manager showed us with pride the flowers in the front window of the hotel which had been arranged, for those with an eye to see them, in the form of a V for Victory for the whole of the occupation.

We got back into our jeep and set off round the corner to the Place Vendome and the Ritz Hotel where we found a different situation and had a long-awaited and good lunch before returning to the Battalion.

CHAPTER V

The Advance through Holland and Germany to the Elbe – 1944–1945

Whilst the Guards Armoured Division was racing forward to liberate Brussels, 6th Guards Tank Brigade spent the first week training with the 3rd Division near Vire in Normandy in some degree of frustration. An incident with the Commanding Officer was somewhat typical of our relationship. As a result of our success against the SS Panthers at Chênedollé, there was some talk on his part to the effect that 'Charles has shown us how to do it'; nevertheless, we seldom saw eye to eye. One morning I received a note from the Adjutant, Vernon Erskine-Crum, on a very minor administrative matter which I thought ill-advised and had dropped him a line to suggest it might be changed. Vernon passed my note to the Commanding Officer who, furious, sent for me and told me that if he had any further questioning of orders which were in fact his, he would not hesitate to send me back to England. I was amazed and thought the matter was being blown up out of all proportion. Indeed, he appeared extremely edgy, but I apologized and the matter was not referred to again.

After a week, the Battalion moved across the Seine by

OPERATIONAL ROUTES OF THE
6TH GUARDS TANK BRIGADE
1944–1945

Scale of Miles

0 20 40 60 80 100 120

Route of Brigade
Major Engagements
Places Liberated
International Boundaries

The advance from Normandy to the Baltic.

pontoon bridge, and a further ten days were spent at Les Andelys in more training with the 3rd Division before the move-up began into the narrow salient forged by the advance to Nijmegen and the ill-fated airborne attack at Arnhem. As we moved up along that crowded main artery in the last week of September, the survivors of the airborne troops were coming back in three-ton trucks down the road on their way to England and passed our column of tanks, stationary at that moment. They were greeted with jeers from our tank crews and shouts of 'Some people have all the f. . .ing luck – one battle and home to England'. This may seem – and was – a very shabby reaction towards the survivors of an extremely gallant action, but it expressed forcibly a feeling in the ordinary regimental front-line soldier to the specialist: it would have made better sense had the reaction come from an infantry company and not from a tank squadron.

The Battalion was now based at Eindhoven and took part in a series of operations to widen the salient. This fighting in Holland up to Christmas was, personally for me, for a reason I still cannot explain, the most difficult time of all. There was little sense of achievement in the minor actions to widen the corridor. On two occasions before battle I woke in the middle of the night, got out from under my tank and walked a distance away to be sick – whether from illness or nerves I do not know, but I suspect the latter.

Our first involvement in fighting was for the small Dutch town of Tilburg in an attack with 15th Scottish Division. The attack was a scrappy one, as far as 'S'

*The officers of 'S' Squadron outside Helmond, Holland in December 1944.
L to R: Lt Michael Law, Lt Peter Hickling, Capt Billie Bull, Lt Tony Stevenson,
Major Charles Farrell, Capt Charles Graham, Lt Peter Ward.*

Squadron was concerned, with the church tower at Tilburg the subject of much tank fire as we believed it was being used as an observation post to bring down shellfire on our accompanying Scottish infantry. Near the end of our advance on the town there was a long railway embankment held by the Germans, but with one tunnel-like gap in it and a bridge across the canal at the other end. The fighting ended with the Germans withdrawing from the town.

The day after the advance to Tilburg I was told that I should have pushed a troop through that tunnel in the railway embankment before our infantry got up. I disagreed, as a water obstacle lay just beyond and the leading tank would have been an all-too-easy target for the enemy anti-tank guns which certainly would have been covering that opening. In any case, the Germans withdrew and Tilburg fell into our hands.

An incident on the way to Tilburg had lost us our hull gunner. Each tank had on the rear panel two smoke dischargers operated from within the tank to provide an emergency smoke screen when moving away from an attack and only to be used when the tank was actually moving. Once the button was pressed the smoke discharge continued until exhausted. The only time they were used was during this advance on Tilburg when my own tank was stationary under shellfire and my hull gunner, in a momentary loss of nerve, pressed the emergency smoke button.

The effect was traumatic for the crew as the engine fans in the prevailing wind sucked the thick smoke directly into the inside of the tank, and in the choking fumes I ordered the crew to get out as quickly as possible. Leaving the driver and hull gunner to recover the tank when the smoke died down, I ran across to another squadron tank with my turret crew, Sgt McInder and Sgt Adair, turned out the Sergeant and his crew and told them to go across and bring my tank forward when it was possible to get into it again.

My hull gunner, who had been responsible for all the trouble, when I saw him that evening was still trembling and obviously in no state to continue. He was sent back to the Forward Delivery Squadron which held the Battalion reinforcements and was replaced. We were very sad to lose him as he was an excellent cook and always seemed to be able to lay his hands on a potato or onion, to improve the bully beef in the 14-man pack on which we lived, and could make of it a very reasonable corned beef hash.

Later in October, the Battalion was involved with 15th Scottish Division in holding a German attack which had come in against the US 7th Armoured Division. US opposition there was weak against the counter-attacking German troops. When we first arrived on the scene, the US Infantry were pulling back in some disorder. Some of them were shouting that there were '50,000 Heinies between us and the river'. In fact there were none. I quote this story to illustrate the point I have made elsewhere that there were good elements and poor elements in all the formations fighting in North-West Europe.

The following day one particular enemy unit from Para Group Hubner had established itself in a good defensive position, and 'S' Squadron was ordered to provide one troop of tanks – Peter Hickling's – to support a somewhat ill-thought out attack in the late afternoon by a company of the 2nd Argyll and Sutherland Highlanders. It was grossly unsuitable tank country and the tanks could only move forward on the one raised concrete road above the waterlogged ground. The nut proved a hard one to crack and the small force had to withdraw leaving one tank bogged down as it tried to turn and the other two reversing slowly down the concrete road with the company of Argyll and Sutherland Highlanders moving level with them. There was eventually nothing I could say over the air to help direct the little battle, so I took my scout car as far forward as I could, then walked up to Peter Hickling's tank to have a word. It was dusk now, and he was energetically waving the infantry back in line with his tank, while the Germans from the Para Group were launching quite a significant small counter-attack. Peter's frantic waving to the infantry to keep in line turned rather incongruously into a smart salute as he saw who it was standing by his tank trying to attract his attention.

There was little to be done, and the two tanks and the Argyll and Sutherland Highlanders company got safely back having inflicted quite heavy casualties on the temporarily advancing Germans. I realized later that I should have ordered Peter Hickling to engage and destroy our bogged and abandoned tank. The fire would have lit up the battle in our favour and obviated any risk of the tank actually being taken over and its armaments used against us. Second thoughts in war, however, come too late, but my negligence was not seized on by the enemy who withdrew overnight and the tank was recovered intact without difficulty. The Squadron could have pulled it without help, but Battalion Headquarters insisted on sending an armoured recovery vehicle – an action which we regarded as unnecessary interference in 'our' battle!

In November, when this particular alarm had subsided and for the first time since the Battalion had left England, a Battalion Officers' Mess was established at Helmond – a clear illustration of the essential independent nature of the operations of the three tank squadrons, which I have mentioned earlier. On one of the first days at Helmond, I fainted in the mess one afternoon and was found to be suffering from dysentery and taken to hospital. Luckily, drugs – I think M & B – worked swiftly and I was back with the Battalion in two days without missing any action. It was also during this period that there was a particularly rowdy party in the Officers' Mess to welcome our old friend, Archie Crabbe, now transferred to the RAF Regiment, who came to have dinner with us. He had been one of the original company commanders in the newly formed 3rd Battalion in 1940. Like some others of the pre-war Scots Guards officers, he had proved at his age, not to be too suitable front-line material. He was however a most delightful and outspoken officer and we were all very fond of him. At this party, one of my troop commanders, Tony Stevenson, threw an apple at a friend across the room. The friend ducked and the apple narrowly missed the Commanding Officer. He was understandably annoyed, and the next day I was sent for and was told that I was failing to keep my young officers under control. It was shortly after this incident that he told Hugh Kindersley, our former Commanding Officer, that of the squadron commanders, Alan Cathcart and John Mann were 'magnificent', but I, although 'good in battle' was 'administratively weak', although I must say in a subsequent letter, after the fighting up to the Rhine, he wrote to Hugh Kindersley that 'all three Squadron Commanders were magnificent'.

Too much attention should not be paid to this. 'Magnificent' was a word he used very often in his citations, and from this point of view he certainly did the Battalion very well indeed. We were doubly fortunate during our campaign in 1944/45 that casualties were low compared with the experience in the two Scots Guards infantry battalions, and decorations in our battalion were more generously distributed. The 1st Battalion fought through Norway, Tunisia and Italy, and 30 of its officers and 334 of its other ranks were killed; the 2nd Battalion fought through the Western Desert, Tunisia, Italy and Germany and 41 officers and 377 other ranks were killed; the 3rd Battalion fought for the ten months' campaign from Normandy to the Baltic, and, of its officers, 12 were killed with 74 other ranks. Nevertheless, the decorations it was awarded were at the same level as the other two battalions.

Perhaps the most striking statistic showing the difference between infantry and armour is that provided in the last eight weeks of the campaign in Western Europe during fighting across the Rhine up to the German surrender. The newly reformed infantry battalion, 2nd Battalion Scots Guards, came from England in March 1945 to replace the 1st Battalion Welsh Guards (whose losses had been too great for them to continue). During the six weeks' fighting up to the German surrender, which brought the 2nd Battalion up to the Elbe, they lost 9 officers and 76 other ranks killed in action, while 17 officers and 248 other ranks were wounded – a total of 350 casualties. In the same six weeks in our tank battalion, one officer and seven other ranks were killed and a handful were wounded.

Casualty statistics do not lie and do reflect the bitterness of the fighting. The spread of the award of decorations after battle can be misleading: the lower the rank, the more likely it is that the award reflects personal bravery. Outstanding action by an infantry or armoured unit as a whole is likely to result in awards at Battalion Commander or Company/Squadron Commander level. All those who fight in the heat of battle deserve recognition, and it is sad that there can be no special award for them.

To return to the story of the Battalion. Due to the influence of Jimmy Gault (a Scots Guardsman who was Military Assistant to the Supreme Commander), General Eisenhower came to visit us at Helmond in early December. While going around my squadron's tanks, he commented to me on the thickness of the armour. I agreed, but pointed out that our designers' failure to slope the armour at an angle did much to negate its thickness and that it was no protection against the German 88. The incident is captured in the photograph on page 114. The potatoes on the track guard are about to be prepared for our crew lunch!

Helmond, Holland, December 1944. General Eisenhower with Major Charles Farrell. The track plates welded on the front of the tank are to give additional protection.

The Ardennes offensive in December 1944 interrupted our pre-Christmas festivities. The Germans achieved a near complete breakthrough, and Eisenhower was forced to give command of the whole northern flank, including the US Divisions involved, to Montgomery who immediately took control of the battlefield in his own inimitable way. 6th Guards Tank Brigade moved south, together with two armoured divisions and two infantry divisions in order to ensure that the Germans did not cross the Meuse. In fact, they did not get quite as far as the river, and we were engaged in mopping-up operations on the flank. It was unfortunate that Montgomery's tact did not match his military ability, and he let it quite clearly be seen what he thought of American strategic generalship.

There began a time of order and counter-order for an attack near Geilenkirchen the first time we crossed the border into Germany. The weather was bitterly cold and the snow was lying thickly on the ground. We painted our tanks white in an effort to camouflage them and discovered that the ground was too hard for us to dig our usual pits under the tanks at night. While near Geilenkirchen, our Squadron's tanks parked alongside a railway station platform became the subject of interest to three 'Rockphoons' (RAF Typhoon fighters equipped with rockets) which ignoring our smoke signals, strafed us repeatedly. We, the tank crews, took refuge in a cellar just below the level of the station platform. We sat there gossiping and exchanging views on the RAF planes above while the strafing continued on our tanks, which we could just see through an opening high up in the cellar wall. I remember that in the middle of one conversation I found my knees were knocking – a phenomenon I had not experienced before – so I quickly crossed them and went on with what I hoped was encouraging talk and prayed that no-one had noticed. Luckily the 'Rockphoons' missed all our tanks. We had survived another example of what is now called 'friendly fire', something which is sadly inevitable in war.

I now had an enjoyable break for forty-eight hours in Brussels. John Mann and I drove there together and stayed at a very comfortable hotel near the Grand Place. My overwhelming memory is of long hot baths, the first since we had landed in Normandy the previous summer. The Belgians welcomed us warmly, and had John not been newly married and I in love with a girl in Devon, the forty-eight hours might have been even more eventful.

Operation VERITABLE

Launched on 8 February 1945, aiming to break through the northern Siegfried Line and destroy the German forces up to the line of the River Rhine.

The marshalling of heavy British and Canadian forces of five Divisions supported by armoured brigades was masterly, and although Montgomery acted with great tactlessness in his relations with the American High Command there was nothing, in our view, wrong with his generalship. We were always very happy that he was our Commander-in-Chief.

The role of 15th Scottish Division was to attack through the Siegfried Line on the flat land between the Rhine and the Reichswald Forest. They were to be supported by 6th Guards Tank Brigade, and we in our turn in 'S' Squadron were as usual to support our friends, 2nd Battalion the Argyll and Sutherland Highlanders. The major problems were the thickly-laid minefields, the very low-lying ground which could be and certainly would be flooded, and the Reichswald Forest which overlooked us.

Whilst talking to the assembled Squadron the evening before the attack, I reminded them that we had never failed to take our objectives, and that tomorrow, for the first time, we would be well into Germany and by the end of the day occupying the high ground overlooking the city of Cleve.

The first day did not, in fact, turn out quite as we had planned it. The flail tanks, which were supposed to beat a way for us through the minefields, bogged down on the approach march, not for the first time, and were never seen. The whole of the leading wave of the Argyll and Sutherland Highlanders were held up by the minefield, and numbers of men were lost attempting to find a way through. There was a line of wounded Argylls showing where the line of the minefield began, which we knew to be a combination of anti-tank and anti-personnel mines. We also discovered to our cost that some 500-lb aerial bombs had also been buried and one of these in the path of the Squadron on our left blew up a troop leader's tank, Colin Campbell's, killing him and all his crew.

Fortunately, my leading right-hand troop leader, Tony Stevenson, spotted what looked like a track leading through the minefield and asked me whether he should have a go at trying to get through on it. At that time I was some 200 yards behind him with the rest of the Headquarters tanks, dispersed for concealment among some crashed British gliders (which had certainly got their route to Arnhem confused!), and I told him to go ahead. He did so with great dash, exploding anti-personnel mines as he went, and the infantry and I, with the rest of the Squadron were successfully able to follow him, the infantry walking carefully in the track marks left by the tanks.

Conditions, however, worsened. The Germans had been busy flooding the area, and as a result many of our tanks became bogged down. However, by towing one another forward, we managed to get five out of our sixteen tanks onto the intermediate objective, the village of Kranenberg. Many prisoners were taken as the opposition was not strong at this stage and obviously from a low-grade German division. In the course of the advance my tank passed close to a concrete gunpit, and as I looked down I saw an 88 mm anti-tank gun pointing directly down our line of advance, but with the canvas jacket still covering the loading mechanism and its unfired rounds stacked neatly behind it. We were fortunate that the German division holding this sector were not of high calibre! We were a very easy target to any resolute anti-tank fire as we floundered in the mud attaching tow ropes and pulling each other forward. Some 300 Germans were taken prisoner, and they trudged back looking pleased to be out of the War. There was shelling from the Reichswald Forest which caused casualties, and as the floods rose only the aerials of our stranded tanks were visible above the water. By evening we had succeeded in taking Kranenberg, our intermediate objective, but only Tony Stevenson's three tanks and two Squadron Headquarters tanks – my own and Sergeant-Major Todd's – had got through onto the firmer ground around the village.

By now it was dark and the infantry commander decided it was not possible to push on to our final objective, the high ground overlooking Cleve.

It did not prove possible to dig the customary pits under our five tanks in order to sleep that night, so we drew up alongside the platform at the railway station where we could sleep with the shelter of the concrete platform above us. I had gone as usual to plan the following day's operation with the Second in Command of the Argyll and Sutherland Highlanders, as Russell Morgan, the Commanding Officer, was away. During the battle I fear I behaved badly towards the Second in Command as he had asked to come up and join me in my tank so we could together control the battle better. I refused his request as I could not have fought the tank with a fourth man in the turret, who would inevitably have been cut in half by the recoil of our 75 mm gun. With hindsight, I think I should have made room for him, possibly by turning out my hull gunner.

Russell Morgan was due back with his battalion the following morning, but with dismay I realized he might not be able to get through the floods to rejoin us. This was a bitter blow, and I lay down to sleep (concerned over the next day's plans) beside a figure asleep under the platform who I took to be a member of my tank crew. I woke to find one of the tank crew with a mug of tea shaking the man next to me; he did not respond and by the light of our torches we found that he was a very dead SS officer in a smart long black uniform coat and highly polished boots.

The morning rapidly improved. When I went up to the top of the station I saw, coming out of the mist and walking along the railway line (the only ground above flood water) the unmistakable figure of Russell Morgan, as always beautifully turned out in his parachute jacket and Argyll bonnet. He never wore a steel helmet. It was also a matter of pride that all tank crews in our brigade, as I have said, wore their black berets at all times rather than the regulation tank helmet.

The feeling of relief at his arrival was all pervading – it suddenly didn't matter so much that we had only got five tanks into the halfway objective of Kranenberg and that the Argyll battalion was depleted, wet and weary on a cold February morning. Before long we were pressing forward again with confidence against a still disorganized enemy, leaving behind the memory among others of the smartly uniformed, dead SS officer and leaving others to identify and bury him, and of a successful attack through the minefields, flooding and fortifications of the far end of the Siegfried Line up to the River Rhine.

At the order group later that day, when we had advanced to the high ground of our original objective outside Cleve, I have a mental picture of Russell Morgan standing up, outlined against the sky, while the company commanders and I sat down as low as we conveniently could and as inconspicuously, conscious of the occasional machine-gun and rifle fire from the nearby buildings of Cleve of which Russell seemed completely oblivious.

Thinking back to him and the outstanding role he played, it is obviously difficult for an outsider to draw a picture of life in an infantry battalion. However, it was portrayed vividly by Martin Lindsay in his diaries published after the War entitled *So Few Got Through*. I have not seen his book mentioned in the bibliographies of the acknowledged writers on the campaign yet it should, in my view, be read, not for its literary merit but for the moving and graphic picture it gives of the stress of life in any infantry battalion in a hard-fought campaign. Martin Lindsay, an MP, was Second in Command of the Gordon Highlanders Battalion in 51st Highland Division for virtually the whole campaign, and perhaps because of his age (he was forty at the time) his diaries are full and balanced.

He is, among other things, very critical of the tank support his battalion received in many of their engagements. While on 48-hour leave in February 1945 he tells how he found himself sharing a room in the Palace Hotel in Brussels with Major Spens of the 2nd Argyll and Sutherland Highlanders (the battalion which 'S' Squadron were so often together with in battle). Lindsay says he (Spens) praised the 6th Guards Tank Brigade which supported them and said they would go anywhere with them, even through woods by moonlight. Lindsay's reply was that he wished they had been with him.

An even better picture of the life of a young officer in battle is given by Archie Elliott, a platoon commander in the 2nd Battalion Scots Guards from 1943 to 1945. His book *Esprit de Corps* is based on his diaries written at the time and has a moving realism. Archie Elliott, now a retired Scottish Judge, Lord Elliott QC MC, was eventually persuaded to publish in 1996. Ludovic Kennedy, after reading it, told me it was the first book that made it clear to him what it was like to fight as an infantry officer in the Second World War.

Published only last year an autobiography of Ian Fraser contains War chapters of a realism that matches those in *Esprit de Corps*. His Scots Guards platoon showed in Italy right up to the end of the campaign and the War, the same 'indomitable fighting spirit'.

Those writers who have denigrated the fighting spirit of the British Army in the closing year of the War in Europe, and they are many, should read these books and the sustained heroism they disclose. It happens that by chance these two books are about the two infantry battalions of my own regiment, the Scots Guards. It is certain that their accounts of courage and steadfastness would be duplicated many times over if platoon commanders in other fighting regiments had committed their memoirs to paper – for most of them time has run out.

The Advance to the Rhine

The next four weeks saw heavy fighting while the British and Canadian divisions fought their way up to the line of the River Rhine. The capture of Cleve was the first

German city which had fallen to the Second Army, we were in Germany itself and now that it was noticeable that the reinforcements which had poured in from across the Rhine fought effectively and with great determination – many of them paratroopers.

After initial fighting in support of 15th Scottish Division and the Argyll and Sutherland Highlanders, we found ourselves attacking in the next phase with the Canadian 7th Infantry Brigade. It was our first experience of working with Canadian troops. The officers above company commander level seemed, in our eyes, old and perhaps not too well attuned to the pressures which we were under. On the other hand, the junior officers and the men were first class and fought hard and well in this very tough fighting up to the Rhine.

In the phase of the attack with the Canadian Infantry Brigade towards Calcar, casualties were not high among the tanks, but we met the heaviest enemy shelling which we had ever encountered, mainly from across the Rhine and as always the infantry suffered much more than us. The Canadian infantry were in Kangaroos – armoured infantry tracked carriers in use for the first time in a major attack – and were not accustomed to our battle tactics. The Germans fought well, and Montgomery has described it as some of the hardest fighting in the whole of the campaign in North-West Europe.

At one moment in the attack with the Canadians moving along the edge of a dark pinewood, a German self-propelled gun down a ride was attempting to turn to bring its gun to bear on my tank. I ordered Sergeant McInder, my tank gunner, to traverse left to engage and then felt the turret come to a grinding halt. I went to lean out of the back of the turret to try to identify the trouble, somewhat reluctantly as the shelling was heavy, when I suddenly realized that a figure was clambering up the back of my tank. This was Sergeant-Major John Todd carrying a heavy track plate hammer. Standing in full view for what seemed an age, he swung the hammer against the bent plate of the storage box on the back of the tank, which an earlier shell had dislodged. At the fifth or sixth attempt, the box broke off allowing the turret to move. The German self-propelled gun was still in difficulties turning in the narrow ride, and Sergeant McInder was able to get in one shot before it moved back into the depths of the wood. The only award I was able to get my quite exceptional Sergeant-Major, to whom I and the whole squadron owe a great debt of gratitude was the French Croix de Guerre, which I think he regarded with a certain distrust. In this engagement we also for the first time were able to engage effectively with our Besa fire numbers of German Infantry moving in the shadows of the wood. It was rare for us to see German infantry in action as they had usually either been firing from concealed positions, or coming forward to surrender.

The Canadian infantry whom we were supporting were at first understandably unwilling to dismount from their Kangaroos and dig in. However after a short time they began to leave their Kangaroos and under the direction of their officers to dig the slit trenches which were so vital to their survival.

On our right, John Mann's Squadron had the same problem and in his case his Liaison Captain, Roger Burnett, heroically in the heavy shell fire, went round from Kangaroo to Kangaroo encouraging the Canadian Infantry to dismount. He was eventually successful but in the end was almost inevitably killed by the shellfire and was then run over and crushed by a Kangaroo to add to John Mann's distress in identifying him.

We 'laagered' for the night in a small group of farm buildings far forward at the furthest point of our advance in order to give the infantry close support. After an hour or so we were again heavily shelled just as I was getting out of my tank turret, having gone back to fetch my map case. The blast of a shell half knocked me back into the tank. I heard cries for help and it was obvious to me that there were casualties. By this time I was tired and it took what seemed like minutes to recover myself to go to the wounded. Others had arrived first and this is an episode of which I am not particularly proud, but I was glad to have been in time to be able to hold the hand of the badly wounded sergeant as he died. Shortly afterwards the transport with our petrol and ammunition reached us. Our supply side was always meticulously arranged and organized by Chips Mclean, the Commander of Headquarter Squadron. On this occasion the Regimental Sergeant-Major, RSM Brown, had come up with the supply column and stood on top of my tank taking the petrol cans passed up to him and filling up the tank, whilst keeping going a loud flow of cheerful talk to anyone within earshot.

Our next advance was with a battalion of the King's Own Scottish Borderers of 3rd Division. It was, for 'S' Squadron, a frustrating attack on Winnekendonck. We were bottled up in a wood, which had been badly chosen as our line of advance with the infantry battalion, and a huge crater at the exit of the wood prevented us fulfilling our role and left Right Flank Squadron to attack Winnekendonck with a battalion of the Lincolns, which they did with great success in the face of heavy opposition. Our time in the wood was an unpleasant one for the infantry as there was sniping and machine-gun fire from neighbouring houses. However, we could find no way for our tanks to debouch from the wood with its old and densely planted trees, and this was to be the last of our engagements before the Rhine crossing.

The Rhine Crossing

It was satisfactory that we were chosen to be the leading tanks to cross the Rhine to join up with and support 6th Airborne Division and the US 17th Airborne Division – a role, we were told, was first allotted to the Guards Armoured Division. It was a far cry from the early days before the Normandy landing when 6th Guards Tank Brigade was to be 'taken out of the war' on Montgomery's orders. He subsequently paid many generous tributes to the Brigade, but his best tribute was the choice of the Brigade to lead the British armoured attack over the Rhine to join up with the airborne divisions.

The Commanding Officer and the squadron commanders – Alan Cathcart, John Mann and I – flew back to

England to liaise with 6th Airborne Division, and we had an intense forty-eight hours with them in detailed planning.

On a fine spring night on 24 March 1945, we went down to the banks of the river and drove onto the rafts, which were towed across the Rhine with little ground opposition, thanks to the airborne landing. The air drop and glider landing had been successful and we joined up without undue difficulty, although sadly realizing that 6th Airborne Division Paratroopers had suffered heavy casualties in hand-to-hand fighting with a German para brigade already in place. Parachutes, with the bodies of our men suspended from them, were still hanging from trees as we advanced through the woods.

Twenty-four hours after the crossing, the role of the Brigade was changed and we were put under command of Ninth US Army. This followed a meeting between Montgomery, General Ridgway, the US Airborne Corps Commander, and General Simpson, the US Ninth Army Commander under whom we now came. The plan was to make a rapid breakout towards Munster carrying the American paratroops of 515th Parachute Regiment on our tanks. 6th Guards Brigade was to operate for the first time under its own Brigadier and not in support of an infantry division: we became in effect an armoured brigade battle group. 'S' Squadron was to carry and to have under its command a company of 515th US Parachute Regiment who hailed from Texas. The US Captain, the Company Commander whom I carried on my tank, was an agreeable professional and relaxed officer who had lately been discharged from hospital having been badly wounded in the Pacific.

The advance on the first day with the American Paratroop Company riding on the tanks was not too heavily opposed, and we made good progress towards Munster some 50 miles away. On the second day, advancing in formation across open country, the Squadron came under heavy fire from a battery of 88 mm guns from a wood to our left front. I saw that one of our tanks in the right-hand troop had been knocked out and was burning, and an 88 mm shot gouged a furrow of earth alongside my own tank. Our position was not a healthy one, and I always had in the back of my mind memories of the disaster at Caumont.

I ordered the Squadron to fire smoke shells to create a screen while we found a way round the flank. The smoke was very effective but two of the troops, instead of moving to the left flank, went back to the village we had just left. I realized that it was not always easy to carry out a controlled withdrawal and flanking movement, but it was in fact the first time we had carried out such a manoeuvre since we landed in Normandy. My temper was not improved by the US Paratroop Second in Command who said, as I got out of my tank to speak to him, 'Well, Major, that was just the prettiest manoeuvre I've ever seen'.

The pressure was maintained by a night march still carrying the US Paratroop company to the communications centre of Dorsten. Just before dawn, a rare German motorized supply column approached our column on a converging road unaware of our presence. We opened fire as the head of the column approached our tanks, the German vehicles were rapidly destroyed and the road became one line of flames. It was difficult to enforce the order to cease the enthusiastic firing – mainly by our Besa machine-guns.

Dorsten was captured the next morning, and for the first time the Battalion featured on the BBC 1 o'clock news. 'The Scots Guards of 6th Guards Armoured Brigade, commanded by Brigadier Greenacre, have captured the town of Dorsten.' It was in this fighting that Harry Pember, the immensely courageous leader of the Battalion Reconnaissance Troop, was killed.

Mathew Ridgway was the only Corps Commander we saw among us during an advance. Otherwise the only officer of a rank senior to us to visit us at the sharp end when we were advancing was Willie Whitelaw, our Battalion Second in Command. On this day we paused with our American friends around a group of farm buildings. Willie arrived with his usual 'Simply splendid! Simply splendid!' and a characteristic wave of the hand. Perhaps because his scout car had been seen, fairly accurate shelling started of the house where we were talking and we continued our conversation under a stout wooden dining-room table until the shelling stopped. As we came out of the house there was a short burst of machine-gun fire. One of our Squadron tank crew, while clambering up a slope had dropped his Sten gun. This unreliable weapon (rejected incidentally by the German Army before the War) had gone off, as it was apt to do, wounding another of our guardsmen in the leg.

This advance with the US paratroopers from the Rhine to Munster was the first time that the Battalion had operated as an integrated battle group with the command resting with the tank formation – rather than, as always before, with the three individual tank squadrons operating in battle independently from their own Battalion HQ in support of, or under command of, the infantry battalion involved. We all understood our new role and it worked well.

The day's advance across rolling wooded country was not strongly opposed. We had become adept and highly trained over the months at by-passing strongpoints, and, if necessary calling down fire from our invaluable supporting artillery.

On 31 March the Squadron was manoeuvring to try and by-pass a strongpoint in the edge of a wood, but, one tank having been knocked out, it looked to me necessary for the Squadron on my left to come round the undefended flank and turn the position.

Our Battalion wireless net worked very well and all the tank commanders were trained to a tight professional discipline. On this occasion, there was a rare breakdown in communication with Battalion Headquarters and the advance was delayed for a time.

The next day I was for the first time in the campaign enjoying myself in our rapid advance. White sheets were hanging out of the windows of the houses, and as we passed, our American Paratroop friends – who were a very 'bouncy' lot – were shooting from the backs of our tanks at anything that showed itself. I thought of Christopher

Marlowe: 'Is it not passing brave to be a King and ride in triumph through Persepolis?'

The normal position of the four tanks of the HQ Troop was immediately behind the leading troop but I was at the time, unusually, the leading tank of the advance along the road as our two forward tank troops were deployed on either side of the village, moving in parallel. On coming round the corner, I saw facing us fifty yards away a German Mark IV tank in the middle of the street, not the most formidable opponent, but carrying a 75 mm gun which could have dealt with us. We immediately halted and engaged it. Our 75 mm armour-piercing shot hit centrally on its turret, did not penetrate and ricocheted straight up in the air. We watched the tracer disappear upwards with dismay. There was no reply from the German tank. We fired again with more success and as we got closer we realized that it had in fact been abandoned, having probably run out of petrol. We moved thankfully round it and on through the village.

We were now on the outskirts of Munster and ready to launch an attack with the Scots Guards and the US Para Regiment in the lead. The first attack was held up by blown bridges, but a way around to the north was possible and 'S' Squadron and its company of Paratroops set off in line ahead.

Just after we started our engine and began to move, I was pleasantly surprised to see our Brigadier, Douglas Greenacre standing at the side of the road, with our Commanding Officer. I and the other tank commanders saluted smartly as we passed the Brigadier. I noticed that he did not give the casual acknowledgment which was the recognized response, but gave each Tank Commander in turn a full regimented salute. We were all gratified by this but it crossed my mind to wonder whether he knew something we did not know of the strength of the impending opposition.

In fact we found our way to our objective unopposed except for occasional small-arms fire. We had however passed close to a German strong point on the edge of the city, which held its fire until the tail of our column reached them, when they opened fire and knocked out the rearmost tank of Tim Gilpin's troop.

Shortly afterwards, on the outskirts of the city, my last contact with the US Paratroop Captain was while we were reconnoitring our next move and looking at a map with our heads close together, when a bullet passed directly between us and hit the tree behind. My feeling of vulnerability was always heightened when the 'shell' of my tank was removed, and my already high regard for the infantry increased. They lived with so much greater danger than we did.

At the moment Munster was being occupied talks were taking place between Montgomery on the one side and Generals Bradley and Eisenhower on the other over the future of Ninth US Army, under whose command we still were. It was decided by Eisenhower, against Montgomery's strong advice, that 21st Army Group should lose the American Ninth Army and, therefore, abort its drive towards Berlin, and that Ninth Army should swing to the south and south-west and protect the flank of Bradley's

American Army group who proposed to swing their axis of attack more towards the Southern Redoubt which it was thought Hitler had formed in Bavaria. We now know no such Redoubt existed.

It was one of the strategic mistakes of the campaign which, it has emerged, Eisenhower made after direct consultation with Stalin, and allowed the Russians to get to Berlin before us with the political difficulties that brought in its train. It affected us on the ground because the American airborne troops left us and we reverted to the command of Second Army. There was not enough strength left in 21st Army Group without 9th US Army to enable it to do more than push up to the line of the Elbe. Although the strategic mistake was certainly Eisenhower's, perhaps if Montgomery had not made himself so intolerable to the American Commanders by his attitude of condescension, he might have been able to influence decisions that were taken. He seemed to take little or no trouble over his vital relationship with the Supreme Commander, except occasionally when prodded by Alanbrooke from London. At the time we, as soldiers at the 'coal face', knew nothing of this, and found Montgomery an inspiring leader.

After we parted with the Americans, the following message was sent to Brigadier Greenacre, commanding 6th Guards Armoured Brigade, by General Matthew Ridgway, Commander of the US Airborne Corps, who later became the Supreme Allied Commander in Europe:

> The period of our joint service has been brief but includes momentous days in a brilliant and now historic operation [the Rhine crossing and the advance to capture Munster].

The contribution of 6th Guards Armoured Brigade in the success of the whole operation has been conspicuously superior.

On the occasions I have been privileged to mingle with elements of your command, I have felt at once that atmosphere, that intangible something almost physical, which only the finest troops create.

I am deeply conscious of having had these incomparable troops in my Corps. I should like to express to you my appreciation of your unfailing and complete cooperation, and my high respect for your professional abilities and leadership.

With the best of good wishes to you and your Brigade. Matthew Ridgway.

Much is written about Anglo-American failures to cooperate – it is good to remember an outstanding success.

It was at this moment that my turn came up in rotation for a week's leave in the UK – the first, of course, which I had had since the Normandy landing. At the end of the day I left the Squadron in a reconnaissance tank, as a protection from small-arms fire, and got back to England via our rear echelon.

My Second in Command, Billy Bull, to whom I handed over, was very much older than the rest of us in his early forties, and it was a magnificent effort on his part to be in a fighting unit at all. I left him in command of the Squadron and I regret bitterly that I took my leave and did not delay it for the few weeks to the end of the campaign. I knew Billy was inclined to be somewhat indecisive if left on his own.

It was a strange sensation to come back to England

directly from the battle and to find life so normal, and to be for a few days with my relations in Scotland where the tenor of life had not changed at all. I was very happy that this should be so, but I felt like a visitor from another world. I went down to London and spent the last two days there with my Devonshire Wren Officer friend with, at that time, our usual bitter-sweet relationship, so I was on balance glad to return to the Battalion.

Tony Stevenson met me at Calais with an enormous German staff car, a Horch, which he had 'liberated'. We drove in great comfort and style back to the Battalion who were at this time between the Weser and the Elbe.

When I got back to the Squadron I found that my Second in Command, Billie Bull had been sent back to the Forward Delivery Squadron (where we held our reserves) for reasons about which I remain unclear. There had been some sharp fighting with some Panzergrenadier reinforcements in and around Uelzen, during which 'S' Squadron had been in reserve.

Billy was something of an icon in the Squadron, always in excellent humour and, in his early forties, that was no mean achievement in the changing conditions. Even the necessarily quick and smooth mounting and dismounting from a Churchill tank for a heavily built and to us middle-aged man was quite an achievement.

Everyone was sad to lose him, not least myself – he had been a very solid support not only to me from the day I took over the Squadron, but to all the others as well. I should not have taken my leave.

The War was now virtually at an end, and as we rested

by the roadside, German staff cars with British motorcycle outrider escorts passed our column of tanks taking the generals to the surrender at Luneberg Heath.

The last time we were under fire was as we came up to the Elbe some German anti-aircraft guns targeted us without success.

After we crossed the river, our final objective was a schloss in the middle of a large estate just south of Lübeck, close to the point at which the British and Russian forces were to join up. As the Squadron arrived at the schloss, moving in extended order across open parkland, we saw to our surprise what appeared to be a weekend party arriving from the opposite direction in smart pony traps carrying well-dressed men and women. My four Headquarters tanks arrived at the courtyard of the schloss almost at the same moment as the pony traps – Sergeant-Major Todd very quickly organized their immediate departure back down the drive.

During this flurry of pony traps being turned around, the owners of the schloss, the Graf and Grafin, came out to greet us speaking excellent English: old 1939 *Tatlers* and *Country Lifes* had been placed on the hall table and the Graf said he wished to give us all hospitality and asked us to be 'free' with his wine cellar. I told him that he and his wife would be allowed to stay in the house provided they moved up to the top floor, and that we would occupy the remainder. Our orders were, in fact, that we must on no account share a house with German nationals, but I felt this unduly harsh in this very large house.

After an hour or so, one of the officers came to me and

said, 'Come and see what we've found!' About 500 yards from the schloss there was a barbed-wire entanglement surrounding a large barn complex in which the slave labour working on the estate was kept under armed guard. There were some two or three hundred in this barn in conditions of unspeakable filth under the supervision of guards equipped with whips and guns. The men who first found the small 'concentration camp' disarmed the 'guards' and opened the gates but the inmates were at this stage too terrified to emerge.

I went back to the schloss, sent for the Graf and asked him how he could tolerate such conditions of slave labour within a few hundred yards of the comfort in which he himself was living. His reply was, 'Major, you don't understand. These people are animals – they can only be treated like animals.' I turned him and his wife out of the house, and the last we saw of them was walking down their long drive each carrying a small suitcase. I do not know whether they survived. One of my troop leaders, Tim Gilpin, then drew my attention to a large portrait of the Graf in the hall of the schloss in which the swastika badge in his buttonhole had been hurriedly, but not successfully painted over.

The following day we were ordered over the air to receive the formal surrender of the local area commander, and, sure enough, a German General with two members of his staff, very beautifully turned out, arrived exactly on time the next morning in a small staff car. It was an unexpected role for us, but we presented as formal an appearance as we could, although conscious of our stained battledress against the grandeur of the German General's uniform. We sat him down opposite us at the table we had arranged in the centre of the salon of the schloss, and which Sgt-Major Todd had covered with a grey army blanket thinking it too ornate for such a serious occasion. I told the General of the arrangements of the points where his men were to assemble to hand over their arms. After a story which had started on the beaches of Arromanches the previous summer, earlier in the Tower of London during the Blitz, and perhaps even earlier at the Nazi Party Rally at Nuremberg in 1938 it was a satisfactory ending.

The War was over, and the role of 6th Guards Armoured Brigade finished. There were parades, a farewell to armour, and the Battalion moved back to the neighbourhood of Bonn.

My own last role was to take a detachment of officers and men from the Squadron to join with our Russian friends in a camp for about 12,000 of them in a large Hermann Goering Divisional Barracks. We were to garrison and provide the patrols around the camp. I was to be the joint Commandant with a Russian Naval officer, Captain Vorontsov, who had commanded a submarine prior to his capture in the Baltic. The 12,000 Russian prisoners in the camp were a mixture of soldiers and civilians, the majority being the male and female slave labour who had been employed in the area.

Captain Vorontsov was 'matched' by a NKVD Commissar, Major Lebedev, who attended all my meetings with the Captain, although he did not follow a great deal because the Captain and I had soon found a common language in French, not understood by the Commissar. Captain Vorontsov was a delightful man and I much enjoyed our many talks together. My memories of the camp are of concerts lasting many hours in which I had to sit in the front row with the Russian officers and express polite appreciation of endless monologues and caricatures in Russian of which I did not understand a word, although the songs and dancing were enjoyable.

In addition, there was the excitement of our patrols rushing to the roof of the prison whenever a wisp of smoke was seen. This was an indication that a local still was operating, at which they were adept. After a successful brewing of alcohol, there would be a 'breakout', some of the surrounding German countryside would be terrorized, and complaints would pour in from the local authorities. I would always complain to Captain Vorontsov, and he always replied that he would speak to his people and see if he could not improve their behaviour. The reaction of Major Lebedev was different. 'Major, you have got guns; you only have to shoot these people as they leave the camp. You can easily surround it and see that no-one gets out.' I hate to think of the military and political reactions if I had followed his advice.

Difficulties do occur on the return to normal peacetime military life, particularly when accentuated by a move from armour back to infantry. One morning I received a call from my Second in Command who was with the Squadron, or 'Company' as it was now called, saying that he was having some trouble and would I please return. He told me that an NCOs' drill course had been organized at

Battalion Headquarters and he had, quite properly, put a number of sergeants on it. They were refusing to go, saying that if they were ordered to do so they would all apply to return to the ranks. I found this hard to believe, so got into my jeep and returned to the Company to find a rather tense situation.

It never occurred to me for a moment that I could not reintroduce good order and that the sergeants would not obey me. These were all men I knew very well indeed, and included Sergeant McInder, my own tank gunner. However, when I interviewed them together and individually, I got an absolute blank refusal. I have never completely understood the reason for their bitterness at this drill course, for which they had been nominated, but it may have been in part due to its timing, combined with the fact that the Drill Sergeant, the Senior Warrant Officer concerned, who was to take the course, was not a man who had in any way been actively employed in the fighting during the campaign. However, this is speculation, and I was faced with a situation in which I was likely to have no sergeants in my Company since they had all applied to return to the ranks, which I found they had the right to do.

Luckily, the Battalion at this time was being commanded by the Second in Command, Willie Whitelaw. I rang Willie and told him what was happening. I said the only solution I could see was to cancel the drill course because, although this meant giving way, the alternative might be the beginning of what could develop into an ugly situation. We talked this through for quite a while, and then Willie, typically, with an explosion of 'God damn and blast it', agreed that the drill course should be cancelled, thereby at an early stage in his career showing his judgement and ability to compromise. I told the sergeants concerned about the cancellation and, more importantly, what I expected of them in future. As far as I know there was never any further trouble.

I went back to the Russian camp to find that the process of returning its inmates to Russia had begun. Lists of the first few hundred had been provided by the Commissar to the Commandant, and trucks were organized by us to take them to the station the following day. To our surprise, when the time came next morning to put the men and women into the trucks, many of them refused to move and our men had to use force to make them get aboard so they could get the trains for repatriation to Russia. We felt wretched, but it was not, I think, an analogous case to that of the repatriation of the Cossacks which has received so much publicity. These were Russian citizens who had been in slave labour in Germany, or soldiers who had been captured. Had we refused to send them back, there is no doubt that reprisals would have been taken against our own prisoners of war who were still in the process of coming back to the United Kingdom from Russia and Germany. Nonetheless, I fear their reception in Russia may not have been a pleasant one – we now know this to be so.

I left the camp to return to England before the move of the Russian soldiers and civilians was complete and was presented by the Russians with a certificate of appreciation (see next page):

To the Commander of the English Forces
at the Russian Assembly Centre
Euskirchen
MAJOR FARRELL

CERTIFICATE OF APPRECIATION

The Headquarters of the Russian Assembly Centre, Euskirchen, in the name of the Staff and People of the Centre, express their thanks for his helpful attitude and kindness to the Russian people in our Assembly Centre. We thank him for his kindness, during his short period of duty in the Assembly Centre, in greatly improving the living conditions and food of all the Staff.

In addition during that period the Staff of the Assembly Centre thank him for the series of Concerts and Moving-picture Entertainments, and the great assistance given to us in organising cultural activities.

His help during this short period enabled us to maintain order and good discipline in the Assembly Centre – therefore the Staff of the Assembly Centre express to Major Farrell their thanks which deserve the widest attention.

Three Signatures

Russian Liaison Officer
with the British 6th Brigade
Major Lebedev

Commandant of the Russian Assembly Centre
Captain Vorontsov

Deputy Commandant of the
Russian Assembly Centre
Captain Schmatkov

15 July, 1945

Before I left and said goodbye, Captain Vorontsov asked me for a testimonial and my address in England – I, of course, wrote out both. I fear they may not have been of much use to him. I only hope and pray that he got back safely to his family at Simferopol in the Crimea.

The years I had served in the Scots Guards had been very happy ones, and the friends I made there have continued to be close, even writing this fifty-five years later. The 3rd Battalion Scots Guards was home during the campaign in North-West Europe to an extraordinarily able group of young men, many of whom were to make their mark in the post-war years.

They number a Deputy Prime Minister, an Archbishop of Canterbury, a Chief Scout and Lord Chamberlain, five heads of major or public companies, one full General and four other Generals, and, perhaps more predictably, four Lord Lieutenants and doubtless others whose achievements since the War are less publicly known. It is salutary to remember that had the third Tank Battalion remained infantry and had the same exposure to war as the two infantry battalions of the Regiment, then the lives of some two-thirds of those referred to above would have almost certainly been marked only by a simple headstone in an immaculately tended War Graves Commission Cemetery in a foreign land.

Apart from the happy memory of forming part of such an exceptionally fine fighting battalion, my dominant memory is of the infantry battalions of the various regiments with whom we fought in cooperation during the campaign. It is difficult to choose, but I would single out three in particular: 2nd Battalion the Argyll and Sutherland Highlanders, whom we were so often with under their inspiring Commanding Officer, Russell Morgan, were tough, dour and utterly reliable; 1st Battalion Welsh Guards in their last battle in the Normandy campaign, having suffered a serious level of casualties in officers and men, still fought with utter and dedicated professionalism at Chênedollé and Le Bas Perrier; and finally, the US paratroopers of the 515th Regiment – their bounding high spirits and morale in the advance and beyond the Rhine were a true tonic. I wish we had been allowed to cross the Elbe and go on to Berlin with them.

I do not recognize in these formations, nor in the others we fought together with, the elements of a 'flawed instrument' which has become fashionable for many contemporary writers to associate with the British, Canadian and American armies in the campaign in North-West Europe.

Epilogue

In May 1945 I was well placed as a 26-year-old Major with a reasonable war behind me and one of the next in line to go to the Staff College.

The obvious decision would have been to remain for a few years and then see how I felt. On the other hand, I had developed a very lively interest in politics and international affairs. I was reminded at a recent luncheon by my old fellow Squadron Commander, John Mann, that he had frequently called me 'Big Picture' – no doubt from my maddening habit of drawing my friends' attention at every opportunity, to strategic issues. On reflection I did not relish the return to peacetime soldiering – infantry soldiering at that – with tours of royal duties in London. I therefore decided to see if I could get a seat in Parliament. My family in Canada were too far away to discuss my decision with and did not know my world in England. I had not seen them for seven formative years from the age of nineteen to twenty-six.

At the age of twenty-six, with no political backing and limited finance, it was perhaps an over-bold decision. However, I had been much on my own since the age of thirteen and I took the decision quickly. I told the Commanding Officer that I did not wish to take up my

Regular Commission in the Regiment, and although he expressed no regret, he wrote to the Regimental Lieutenant Colonel in London to say, 'I know you will be sorry to learn that Charles Farrell has decided not to take up his Regular Commission.'

My political venture was short-lived. After an interview with the Chairman of the Conservative Party, Henry Brooke, I was placed on the Candidate list for the 1945 General Election. I got as far as one of the last two for the Heston and Isleworth Constituency but they opted for Patricia Hornsby-Smith, who later became an MP and a Government Minister.

I then stood jointly as a Conservative with Ian Orr-Ewing (later also a Conservative Minister) in the LCC election in the autumn of 1945 in the safe labour seat of North St Pancras. As we expected we lost, and I came to the conclusion, no doubt others thought the same, that a political career was not for me.

After a brief business experience which I did not enjoy, I took the Foreign Office entrance and after appropriate interviews I was accepted and in 1947 joined Her Majesty's Foreign Service – now the Diplomatic Service. I spent ten years in it from the age of twenty-seven. These were ten fascinating and rewarding years, in the Far East, during the Korean War and in Europe while the Cold War was at its height.

As a First Secretary in the Brussels Embassy in 1957, I was offered an opportunity to go into British industry, to train briefly and then become Managing Director of British Sidac, a northern manufacturing company. The offer financially was very enticing and after discussing it with my wife during a week in Venice, I resigned from the Foreign Service.

I duly became Managing Director of British Sidac (the first they had), made it into a public company and expanded it mainly by acquisition into a different league and size. The company's progress was then halted in the early 1970s, firstly by the Monopolies Commission and also by profits eroded by the gradual but steady decline, in the face of competition from Plastics of its main product Cellophane. I was glad however in the 1960s to have taken the initiative with ICI to establish a joint plastics company at Wigton, Cumberland which continues to be the base of the prosperity of the town.

I recall the words of that outstanding military historian Sir John Keegan at his 1999 London Library Lecture 'Old Men Forget' when he told how his 'eyes glazed over' at the thought of business 'Takeover' stories. Suffice to say here that I resigned from British Sidac after a Boardroom coup in the early 1970s and with two former colleagues set up over the years three or four 'start-up' companies, one of which was particularly successful and became a public company in due course. We eventually sold it to a television company of which I became a Director. I resigned at the age of 73 in 1992.

I married in 1949 in my early days at the Foreign Office and last year we celebrated our Golden Wedding. My wife and I live peacefully and happily here in Oxfordshire among good friends and with the enormous pleasure of frequent visits from children and grandchildren – my hope and my belief is that they will not have the experiences of war which my generation had over half a century ago.

Appendix I

The following article appeared in the *Spectator* on 31 May 1997 and I had an opportunity in the letter which follows to publicize my views, albeit to a limited audience, which this book now extends.

We can correct the miscarriage of justice. We cannot correct miscarriages of history

BRUCE ANDERSON

The first world war was a second Fall of Man. At the time, it was thought to be the war that would end war. That was the most foolish illusion in human history since Eve and the apple. In reality, it was the war which began wars, and many other evils; it would be naive to suppose that its fecundity has been exhausted.

This is the background to the proposal to pardon the 307 British servicemen executed during that war for cowardice, desertion and similar offences. There would appear to be a strong argument for doing so. We all know, surely, that the first world war was fought by a British Army of lions led by donkeys. To have psychological cases shot for cowardice was characteristic of the way that those dunderhead generals and blimpish officers treated their men. The war was unnecessary; it was also, therefore, unjust. It follows that to put men to death in the name of military justice was a mockery of justice. Moreover, many of those executed were volunteers. Some of them had had excellent service records, until they cracked under intolerable strain. In the second world war, by which time such matters were better understood, there were no executions for cowardice.

It is impossible for the rest of us to imagine what 15 minutes in the front line of the trenches must have been like, let alone the weeks and months that some of those men had spent there, before they faced a firing squad. How can most of us possibly claim that we would have held fast when they fell back; how, then, can we continue to condemn them for cowardice? We cannot restore dead men to life, but even if individuals do not benefit, a pardon would at least repair one fragment of the moral order which was shattered in those terrible years.

There seems to be a powerful argument, an irresistible appeal to our compassion. In reality, it is a sentimental argument; the only appeal is to our self-indulgence.

Unless Britain had been willing to become an island off a German-dominated continent, we had no choice but to stand firm with our allies in August 1914. Had we failed to do so, Germany would have won, and we could have found only one modus vivendi with the German Empire: subjugation. The war that we would have avoided would have had to be fought later, in much less favourable circumstances, with no help from the former allies whom we would have betrayed. Even if the Austro-Hungarian Empire could have survived a German victory, the Russian one would have disintegrated in defeat. We know what monsters 1914–18 brought forth; there is little reason to suppose that a German victory in the 1914–16 war would have had more benign consequences, and a much higher proportion of the monstrousness would have been committed on this side of the Channel.

The war had to be fought, and there are no grounds for arguing that it could have been fought differently. One of the many tragedies of 1914 was that defensive military capabilities were far superior to offensive ones. There was nothing any of the generals could have done about this; nothing that any general in history could have done about it. For an interlude between the decline of cavalry and the fuller development of air power and the tank, there was only one way to win a war on the Western Front: attrition, meaning trench warfare interspersed by hideously bloody offensives.

Youngsters undergoing basic training in the British Army often find themselves on a run, confronting a six-foot jump across a shallow ravine. If, as is natural, they hang back, it will be a split second before a stentorian bellow reminds them what they are trying to become. 'There's only one thing to be afraid of 'ere, lads,' the sergeant will inform them, 'and I'm be'ind her.' All armies have tried to ensure that private soldiers are at least as afraid of their own NCOs as of the enemy. That task was never more vital than during the first world war.

In a good army, at least until a very late stage, a trained soldier's will to fight is sustained by his desire to stand well with his colleagues; fear of shame is a remarkably effective antidote to fear of dying. But a fine soldier does not suddenly turn into a psychological case. There is an intervening phase, which can be shortened if the soldier in question knows that he will receive sympathetic treatment, and extended if he realises that there is no hope of sympathy. Between 1914 and 1918, there was no alternative: that phase had to be extended, even if this meant sending genuine psychological cases to the firing-squad.

It does not impugn the bravery of the men in the trenches to assume that their willingness to endure intolerable stress might have diminished if authority had been more tolerant of their failure to do so. This is, indeed, more than an assumption; it can virtually be proved by reference to the British Army's experiences in 1944/45. In both Italy and Normandy, there was a widespread reluctance to be among the last British casualties of the second world war. Some formations had to be pulled out of the front line because they were unwilling to fight. At the time, the effects of this were mitigated, both by the use of fresh levies – including Americans – and by overwhelming air superiority. But if the battle had been more even and it had been necessary to optimise British resources, it is not clear whether that could have been achieved without resort to the firing-squad.

The BEF knew that anyone trying to soldier no more because he could stand it no longer was heading straight for a court-martial. Few did. But if the rear echelon had offered, not chains and cells, but counselling, how many more men would have given way? Kindness can destroy morale more effectively than harshness can. Three hundred and seven dead men was a tragedy for them and their families; it was also the equivalent of ten minutes' losses on the first day of the Somme. The British Army was the only army that began at the beginning and was still unbroken in November 1918. Given the overriding objective of keeping that army in being as a fighting force, 307 executions was a small price to pay.

We must also remember that to pardon the condemned would mean condemning those who sentenced them. There were, no doubt, examples of atrocious insensitivity, but is anyone claiming that none of the 307 were guilty as charged? There have even been suggestions of a sift through the records and a new adjudication on each individual case. That might be the only fair way to proceed; it would also, if taken seriously, take years, cost millions and still leave huge areas of doubt.

From Ludendorff to Joan Littlewood, the British military authorities of 1914–18 have been subjected to relentless slander. As a result, a false version of the first world war has now become entrenched in the popular consciousness; hence the proposed pardon. But we cannot assuage past sufferings by subjecting past actions to our facile moral judgements. In part, we may be able to correct miscarriages of justice. We cannot correct miscarriages of history.

The following is a letter from Mr Norman in the *Spectator* of 7 June 1997:

Our brave men

Sir: Bruce Anderson's article on pardons for first world war soldiers executed for cowardice (Politics, 31 May) makes no distinction between those unjustly convicted and those justly convicted.

The major case for the blanket pardon, which I hope is successful, is that most of those executed were suffering from psychological illnesses generally known as shell-shock. This was a known and recognised illness at the time these executions occurred, and these men should have been invalided out of the service. Also, in a very substantial number of cases the courts-martial were not conducted in strict accordance with military law. This is in itself more than sufficient grounds to issue pardons.

Mr Anderson's comments justifying the necessity for this draconian regime are equally wide of the mark. First, the British army was not the only army not to crack under the strain; the German army also did not crack. It was finally defeated in 1918, but that is different from cracking.

It is worth noting here that the German army of the first world war did not execute soldiers for cowardice, whereas the French army – which did crack – was notorious even by the standards of its day for executing its soldiers.

The above utterly destroys his argument that this draconian regime had a military necessity. In the second world war the British army did not ever execute soldiers for cowardice; neither did the American army, with only one exception in France near the end of the war. Yet how will Mr Anderson rate the conduct of the American soldiers on Omaha Beach and when stemming the German offensive in the Ardennes? It is generally agreed that their conduct on these occasions was exemplary.

The assertion that British soldiers did not fight with the same gallantry as their fathers in the first world war is the most disgraceful smear on those who gave their lives so that the likes of Bruce Anderson can write his poisonous articles in complete freedom. Yes, Mr Anderson, units sere withdrawn from the front at regular intervals for rest as well as re-manning to make up for casualties. Exactly the same happened in the first world war.

Finally, may I refute the Anderson canard that soldiers need to fear their NCOs more than the enemy. I served for two years in the army and I can assure Mr Anderson that not only did I not fear my NCOs, I never knew anyone who did. Respected and in many cases liked, yes; feared no.

In essence this article was written with little or only garbled knowledge of the subject and appears to have been wholly unresearched. It has done absolutely nothing for the reputation of your magazine.

G.J. Norman,
7 Queens Parade,
Cheltenham,
Gloucestershire.

My reply appeared in the *Spectator* of 21 June 1997:

Executions for cowardice

Sir: The letter from G.J. Norman in your issue of 7 June severely criticises – rightly – Bruce Anderson for his denigration of the British Army's fighting quality in Italy and Normandy in 1944–1945.

I fear Mr Anderson may have been seriously misled by much of the revisionist history of the second world war, perhaps exemplified by Max Hastings in his book *Overlord* in which he greatly underrates the performance of the British fighting soldier in Normandy; he has since been followed by other writers in the same vein.

It is difficult to summarise a complex subject in a brief letter. But, in essence, the truth in my experience was that there were, measured in terms of fighting quality, good, average and poor units and divisions in much the same proportion in the British, American and German armies in north-west Europe (the area with which I was familiar).

The Allies were greatly helped, although very seldom at the point of battle, by overwhelming air superiority. This was counter-balanced by conspicuous German superiority in tanks, anti-tank guns, light machine guns, personal anti-tank weapons and mortars. It was only in artillery that the British were predominant.

In their general organisation for war the Germans also had a significant advantage, employing a far higher proportion of their men as fighting soldiers rather than in a long administrative tail.

I suggest that Bruce Anderson reads, if he has not already

done so, *Esprit de Corps*, the war memoir of W.A. Elliott, a platoon commander in the 2nd Battalion Scots Guards from 1943 to 1945 and now a retired Scottish judge, Lord Elliott QC, MC. His Scots Guards infantry battalion lost in killed and wounded 113 officers and 1,246 other ranks in the course of the second world war – higher casualties than the same battalion suffered in the first world war: a not unusual statistic but one which may surprise some, even among those who have written of the campaigns in Europe in the last war.

The implications in Mr Anderson's article that British soldiers would have fought more resolutely if the death penalty for cowardice had been in place, and that when they did perform well it was due in part to their fear of their NCOs, is ridiculous and offensive.

Charles Farrell,
Cuttmill House,
Watlington,
Oxfordshire.

Index